RASPBERRY PI - 16X2 LCD, 74HC595 SSR, PWM, SERVO-STEPPER-DC MOTOR,TOUCH PAD, MP DETECTOR, H-BRIDGE MOTOR,ESR METER,LIGHT FENCE ALARAM ETC..,

Raspberry Pi - 16x2 LCD, 74HC595 SSR, PWM, Servo-Stepper-DC Motor,Touch Pad, MP Detector, H-Bridge Motor,ESR Meter,Light Fence Alaram etc..,

CONTENTS

ACKNOWLEDGMENTS

The writer might want to recognize the diligent work of the article group in assembling this book. He might likewise want to recognize the diligent work of the Raspberry Pi Foundation and the Arduino bunch for assembling items and networks that help to make the Internet of Things increasingly open to the overall population. Yahoo for the democratization of innovation!

INTRODUCTION

The Internet of Things (IOT) is a perplexing idea comprised of numerous PCs and numerous correspondence ways. Some IOT gadgets are associated with the Internet and some are most certainly not. Some IOT gadgets structure swarms that convey among themselves. Some are intended for a solitary reason, while some are increasingly universally useful PCs. This book is intended to demonstrate to you the IOT from the back to front. By structure IOT gadgets, the per user will comprehend the essential ideas and will almost certainly develop utilizing the rudiments to make his or her very own IOT applications. These included ventures will tell the per user the best way to assemble their very own IOT ventures and to develop the models appeared. The significance of Computer Security in IOT gadgets is additionally talked about and different systems for protecting the IOT from unapproved clients or programmers. The most significant takeaway from this book is in structure the tasks yourself.

1. 16X2 LCD INTERFACING WITH RASPBERRY PI UTILIZING PYTHON

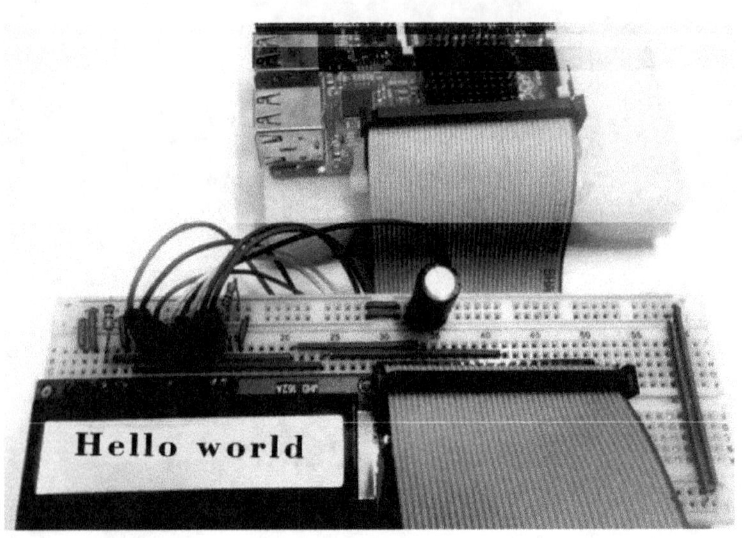

Raspberry Pi is an ARM design processor based board intended for electronic specialists and specialists. The PI is one of most confided in venture advancement stages out there now. With higher processor speed as well as 1 Giga Byte Random Access Memory, the PI can be utilized for some, prominent activities like Image preparing and IoT.

For doing any of prominent ventures, one have to comprehend the fundamental elements of PI. We will cover all the fundamental functionalities of Raspberry Pi in these instructional exercises. In every instructional exercise we will talk about one of elements of PI. Before the finish of this Raspberry Pi Tutorial Series, you will have the option to do prominent activities without anyone else's input. Experience underneath instructional exercises:

- Beginning with Raspberry Pi

- Raspberry Pi Configuration

- Driven Blinky

- Catch Interfacing

- PWM age

- Controlling DC Motor

- Stepper Motor Control
- Interfacing Shift Register

- Raspberry Pi ADC Tutorial

- Servo Motor Control

- Capacitive Touch Pad

In this instructional exercise, we will Control a 16x2 Liquid Crystal Display Display utilizing Raspberry Pi. We will associate the Liquid Crystal Display to (General Purpose Input Output) pins of PI to show characters on it. We will compose a program in PYTHON to send the suitable directions to the LCD through GPIO and show the required characters on its screen. This screen will prove to be useful to show sensor esteems, intrude on status and furthermore for showing time.

There are various sorts of LCDs in the market. Realistic LCD is more mind boggling than 16x2 LCD. So here we are going for 16x2 LCD show, you can even utilize 16x1 LCD in the event that you need. 16x2 LCD has 32 characters altogether, 16 in first line and another 16 in second line. JHD162 is 16x2 LCD Module characters LCD. We have as of now interfaced 16x2 LCD with 8051, AVR, Arduino and so forth. You can discover all our 16x2 LCD related venture by following this connection.

We will examine somewhat about PI GPIO before going any further.

There are 40 GPIO yield sticks in Raspberry Pi 2. In any case, out of 40, just 26 GPIO pins (GPIO2 to GPIO27) can be modified. A portion of these pins play out some uncommon capacities. With extraordinary GPIO set aside, we have 17 GPIO remaining.

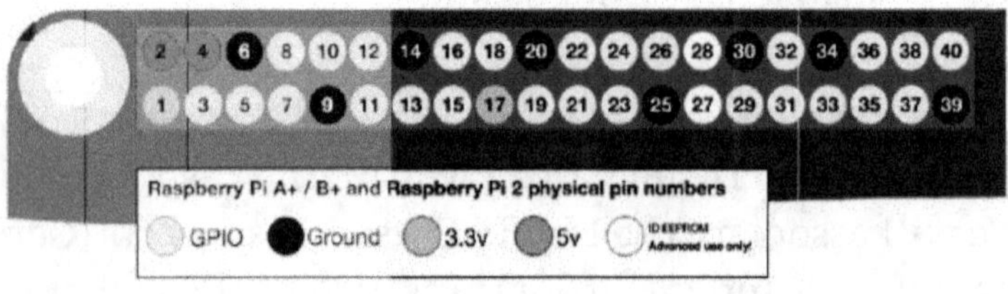

There are +5V (Pin 2 or 4) and +3.3V (Pin 1 or 17) control yield nails to the board, these are for associating different modules and sensors. We are going to control the 16*2 LCD through the +5V rail. We can send control sign of +3.3v to LCD however for working of LCD we have to control it by +5V. The LCD won't work with +3.3V.

To find out about GPIO pins and their present yields, experience: LED Blinking with Raspberry Pi

Components Required:

Here we are utilizing Raspberry Pi two Model B with Raspbian Jessie OS. All the fundamental Hardware and Software prerequisites are recently talked about, you can find it in the Raspberry Pi Introduction, other than that we need:

- Connecting pins
- 16*2 LCD Module
- 1K?resistor (2 pieces)
- 10K pot
- 1000μF capacitor
- Breadboard

Circuit and Working Explanation:

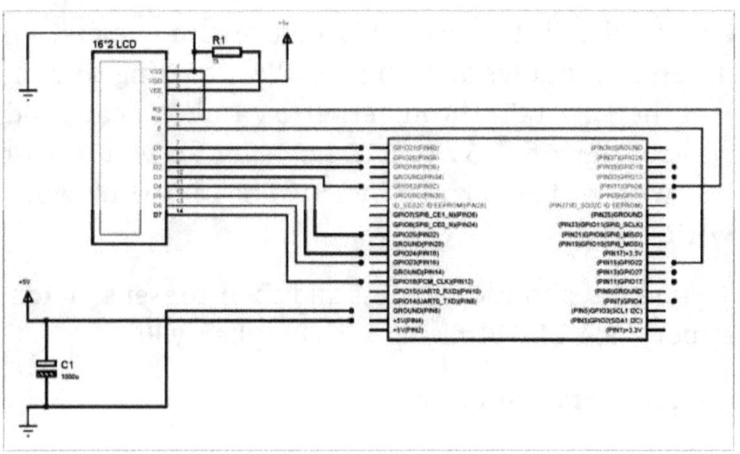

As appeared in the Circuit Diagram, we have Interfaced Raspberry Pi with Liquid Crystal Display show by associating 10 General Purpose Input Output pins of PI to the 16*2 LCD's Control as well as Data Transfer Pins. We have utilized GPIO Pin 21, 20, 16, 12, 25, 24, 23, and 18 as a BYTE and made 'PORT' capacity to send information to LCD. Here General Purpose Input Output 21 is (Least Significant Bit) as well as General Purpose Input Output 18 is (Most Significant Bit).

16x2 LCD Module has 16 pins, which can be separated into five classifications, Power Pins, differentiate pin, Control Pins, Data pins and Backlight pins. Here is the short depiction about them:

Category	Pin NO.	Pin Name	Function

Power Pins	1	VSS	Ground Pin, connected to Ground
	2	VDD or Vcc	Voltage Pin +5V
Contrast Pin	3	V0 or VEE	Contrast Setting, connected to Vcc thorough a variable resistor.
Control Pins	4	RS	Register Select Pin, RS=0 Command mode, RS=1 Data mode
	5	RW	Read/ Write pin, RW=0 Write mode, RW=1 Read mode
	6	E	Enable, a high to low pulse need to enable the LCD
Data Pins	7-14	D0-D7	Data Pins, Stores the Data to be displayed on LCD or the command instructions
Backlight Pins	15	LED+ or A	To power the Backlight +5V
	16	LED- or K	Backlight Ground

We emphatically prescribe to simply experience this article to comprehend the LCD working with its Pins and Hex Commands.

We will talk about quickly the way toward sending information to LCD:

1. E is set high (empowering the module) and RS is set low (disclosing to LCD we are giving order)

2. Giving worth 0x01 to information port as an order to clear screen.

3. E is set high (empowering the module) and RS is set high (revealing to LCD we are giving information)

4. Demonstrating the ASCII code for characters should be shown.

5. E is set low (revealing to LCD that we are finished sending information)

6. When this E pin goes low, the LCD procedure the got information and shows the relating result. So this pin is set to high before sending information and dismantled down to ground subsequent to sending information.

As said we will send the characters in a steady progression. The characters are given to LCD by (American standard Code for Information Interchange) codes. The table of ASCII codes is demonstrated as follows. For instance, to show a character "@", we have to send a hexadecimal code "40". In the event that we give esteem 0x73 to the LCD it will show "s". Like this we will send the fitting codes to the LCD to show the string "HELLO WORLD".

Dec	Hx	Oct	Char	Dec	Hx	Oct	Html	Chr	Dec	Hx	Oct	Html	Chr	Dec	Hx	Oct	Html	Chr
0	0	000	NUL (null)	32	20	040		Space	64	40	100	@	@	96	60	140	`	`
1	1	001	SOH (start of heading)	33	21	041	!	!	65	41	101	A	A	97	61	141	a	a
2	2	002	STX (start of text)	34	22	042	"	"	66	42	102	B	B	98	62	142	b	b
3	3	003	ETX (end of text)	35	23	043	#	#	67	43	103	C	C	99	63	143	c	c
4	4	004	EOT (end of transmission)	36	24	044	$	$	68	44	104	D	D	100	64	144	d	d
5	5	005	ENQ (enquiry)	37	25	045	%	%	69	45	105	E	E	101	65	145	e	e
6	6	006	ACK (acknowledge)	38	26	046	&	&	70	46	106	F	F	102	66	146	f	f
7	7	007	BEL (bell)	39	27	047	'	'	71	47	107	G	G	103	67	147	g	g
8	8	010	BS (backspace)	40	28	050	(	(	72	48	110	H	H	104	68	150	h	h
9	9	011	TAB (horizontal tab)	41	29	051	)	)	73	49	111	I	I	105	69	151	i	i
10	A	012	LF (NL line feed, new line)	42	2A	052	*	*	74	4A	112	J	J	106	6A	152	j	j
11	B	013	VT (vertical tab)	43	2B	053	+	+	75	4B	113	K	K	107	6B	153	k	k
12	C	014	FF (NP form feed, new page)	44	2C	054	,	,	76	4C	114	L	L	108	6C	154	l	l
13	D	015	CR (carriage return)	45	2D	055	-	-	77	4D	115	M	M	109	6D	155	m	m
14	E	016	SO (shift out)	46	2E	056	.	.	78	4E	116	N	N	110	6E	156	n	n
15	F	017	SI (shift in)	47	2F	057	/	/	79	4F	117	O	O	111	6F	157	o	o
16	10	020	DLE (data link escape)	48	30	060	0	0	80	50	120	P	P	112	70	160	p	p
17	11	021	DC1 (device control 1)	49	31	061	1	1	81	51	121	Q	Q	113	71	161	q	q
18	12	022	DC2 (device control 2)	50	32	062	2	2	82	52	122	R	R	114	72	162	r	r
19	13	023	DC3 (device control 3)	51	33	063	3	3	83	53	123	S	S	115	73	163	s	s
20	14	024	DC4 (device control 4)	52	34	064	4	4	84	54	124	T	T	116	74	164	t	t
21	15	025	NAK (negative acknowledge)	53	35	065	5	5	85	55	125	U	U	117	75	165	u	u
22	16	026	SYN (synchronous idle)	54	36	066	6	6	86	56	126	V	V	118	76	166	v	v
23	17	027	ETB (end of trans. block)	55	37	067	7	7	87	57	127	W	W	119	77	167	w	w
24	18	030	CAN (cancel)	56	38	070	8	8	88	58	130	X	X	120	78	170	x	x
25	19	031	EM (end of medium)	57	39	071	9	9	89	59	131	Y	Y	121	79	171	y	y
26	1A	032	SUB (substitute)	58	3A	072	:	:	90	5A	132	Z	Z	122	7A	172	z	z
27	1B	033	ESC (escape)	59	3B	073	;	;	91	5B	133	[	[	123	7B	173	{	{
28	1C	034	FS (file separator)	60	3C	074	<	<	92	5C	134	\	\	124	7C	174			|
29	1D	035	GS (group separator)	61	3D	075	=	=	93	5D	135	]	]	125	7D	175	}	}
30	1E	036	RS (record separator)	62	3E	076	>	>	94	5E	136	^	^	126	7E	176	~	~
31	1F	037	US (unit separator)	63	3F	077	?	?	95	5F	137	_	_	127	7F	177		DEL

Programming Explanation:

Once everything is associated according to the circuit chart, we can turn ON the PI to compose the program in PYHTON.

We will discuss barely any directions which we are gonna to use in PYHTON program,

We are gonna to import GPIO record from library, underneath work empowers us to program GPIO pins of PI. We are likewise renaming "GPIO" to "IO", so in the program at whatever point we need to allude to GPIO pins we will utilize the word 'IO'.

```
import RPi.GPIO as IO
```

In some cases, when the GPIO pins, which we are attempting to utilize, may be doing some different capacities. All things considered, we will get admonitions while executing the program. Beneath direction advises the PI to disregard the admonitions and continue with the program.

```
IO.setwarnings(False)
```

We can allude the General Purpose Input Output pins of PI, either by nail number to board otherwise by their capacity number. Like 'PIN 29' on the board is 'GPIO5'. So we advise here it is possible that we will speak to the pin here by '29' or '5'.

```
IO.setmode (IO.BCM)
```

We are setting 10 GPIO sticks as yield pins, for Data and Control pins of LCD.

```
IO.setup(6,IO.OUT)
```

```
IO.setup(22,IO.OUT)

IO.setup(21,IO.OUT)

IO.setup(20,IO.OUT)

IO.setup(16,IO.OUT)

IO.setup(12,IO.OUT)

IO.setup(25,IO.OUT)

IO.setup(24,IO.OUT)

IO.setup(23,IO.OUT)

IO.setup(18,IO.OUT)
```

while 1: direction is utilized as always circle, with this order the announcements inside this circle will be executed consistently.

The various capacities and directions have been clarified in underneath 'Code' area with the assistance of 'Remarks'.

Subsequent to composing the program and executing it, the Raspberry Pi sends characters to LCD individually and the LCD shows the characters on the screen.

Code

```python
import RPi.GPIO as IO        # calling for header file
which helps us use GPIO's of PI
import time                  # calling for time to provide
delays in program
import sys
IO.setwarnings(False)        # do not show any warnings
IO.setmode (IO.BCM)          # programming the GPIO by
BCM pin numbers. (like PIN29 as 'GPIO5')

IO.setup(6,IO.OUT)                   # initialize GPIO Pins as
outputs
IO.setup(22,IO.OUT)
IO.setup(21,IO.OUT)
IO.setup(20,IO.OUT)
IO.setup(16,IO.OUT)
IO.setup(12,IO.OUT)
IO.setup(25,IO.OUT)
IO.setup(24,IO.OUT)
IO.setup(23,IO.OUT)
IO.setup(18,IO.OUT)

def send_a_command (command):        # execute the
loop when "sead_a_command" is called
  pin=command
  PORT(pin);                         # calling 'PORT' to assign
value to data port
  IO.output(6,0)                     # putting 0 in RS to
tell LCD we are sending command
  IO.output(22,1)                    # telling LCD to receive
command/data at the port by pulling EN pin high
  time.sleep(0.05)
  IO.output(22,0)                    # pulling down EN
```

pin to tell LCD we have sent the data.

```
  pin=0
  PORT(pin);                        # pulling down the port
to stop transmitting

def send_a_character (character):          # execute the
loop when "send_a_character" is called
  pin=character
  PORT(pin);
  IO.output(6,1)
  IO.output(22,1)
  time.sleep(0.05)
  IO.output(22,0)
  pin=0
  PORT(pin);

def PORT(pin):                      # assigning PIN by taking
PORT value
  if(pin&0x01 == 0x01):
    IO.output(21,1)                 # if bit0 of 8bit 'pin' is true,
pull PIN21 high
  else:
    IO.output(21,0)                 # if bit0 of 8bit 'pin' is false,
pull PIN21 low
  if(pin&0x02 == 0x02):
    IO.output(20,1)                 # if bit1 of 8bit 'pin' is true,
pull PIN20 high
  else:
    IO.output(20,0)                 # if bit1 of 8bit 'pin' is true,
pull PIN20 low
  if(pin&0x04 == 0x04):
    IO.output(16,1)
```

```python
  else:
    IO.output(16,0)
  if(pin&0x08 == 0x08):
    IO.output(12,1)
  else:
    IO.output(12,0)
if(pin&0x10 == 0x10):
    IO.output(25,1)
  else:
    IO.output(25,0)
  if(pin&0x20 == 0x20):
    IO.output(24,1)
  else:
    IO.output(24,0)
  if(pin&0x40 == 0x40):
    IO.output(23,1)
  else:
    IO.output(23,0)
  if(pin&0x80 == 0x80):
    IO.output(18,1)          # if bit 7 of 8bit 'pin' is true
pull PIN18 high
  else:
    IO.output(18,0)          #if bit 7 of 8bit 'pin' is false
pull PIN18 low


while 1:
  send_a_command(0x01);          # sending 'all clear'
command
  send_a_command(0x38);          # 16*2 line LCD
  send_a_command(0x0E);          # screen and cursor
```

```
ON
  send_a_character(0x43);        # ASCII code for 'C'
  send_a_character(0x49);        # ASCII code for 'I'
  send_a_character(0x52);        # ASCII code for 'R'
  send_a_character(0x43);        # ASCII code for 'C'
  send_a_character(0x55);        # ASCII code for 'U'
  send_a_character(0x49);        # ASCII code for 'I'
  send_a_character(0x54);        # ASCII code for 'T'


   # ASCII codes for 'WORLD'
  send_a_character(0x44);
  send_a_character(0x49);
  send_a_character(0x47);
  send_a_character(0x45);
  send_a_character(0x53);
  send_a_character(0x54);


  time.sleep(1)
```

2. SERVO MOTOR CONTROL WITH RASPBERRY PI

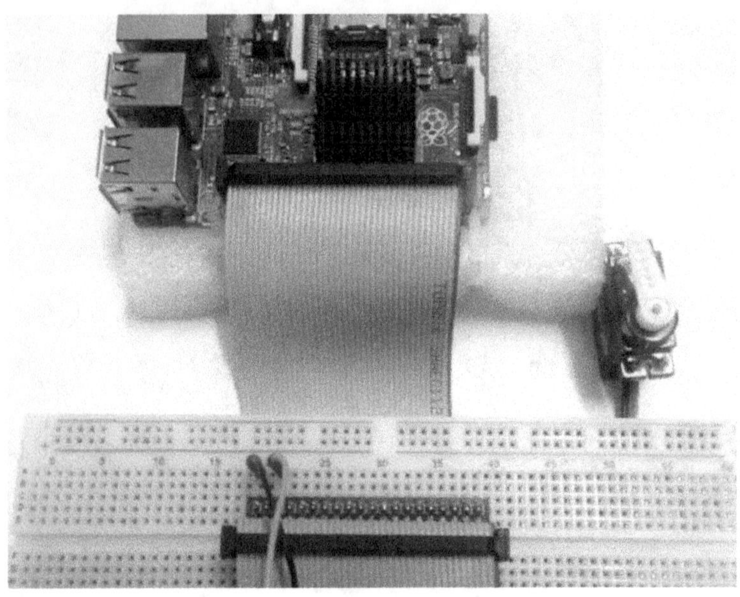

Raspberry Pi is an ARM engineering processor based board intended for electronic designers and specialists. The PI is one of most confided in venture improvement stages out there now. With higher processor speed and 1 GB RAM, the PI can be utilized for some, prominent undertakings like Image handling and Internet of Things.

For doing any of prominent ventures, one have to

comprehend the essential elements of PI. We will cover all the fundamental functionalities of Raspberry Pi in these instructional exercises. In every instructional exercise we will examine one of elements of PI. Before the finish of this Raspberry Pi Tutorial Series, you will have the option to do prominent activities without anyone else. Experience beneath instructional exercises:

- Beginning with Raspberry Pi

- Raspberry Pi Configuration

- Driven Blinky

- Raspberry Pi Button Interfacing

- Raspberry Pi PWM age

- Controlling DC Motor utilizing Raspberry Pi
- Stepper Motor Control with Raspberry Pi

- Interfacing Shift Register with Raspberry Pi

- Raspberry Pi Analog-to-Digital Converter Tutorial

In this instructional exercise we will Control Servo Motor with Raspberry Pi. Before going to servo we should discuss PWM in light of the fact that the idea of controlling Servo Motor originates from it.

PWM (Pulse Width Modulation):

We have recently discussed PWM ordinarily in: Pulse width Modulation with ATmega32 , PWM with Arduino Uno, PWM with 555 clock IC and PWM with Arduino Due. PWM means 'Heartbeat Width Modulation'. PWM is a strategy utilized for getting variable voltage from a steady power supply. For better comprehension PWM consider the circuit underneath,

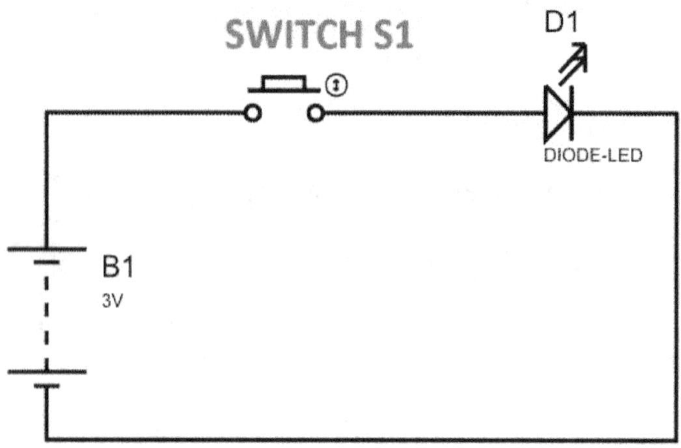

In above figure, if the switch is shut constantly over some stretch of time, the LED will be 'ON' during this time consistently. On the off chance that the switch is shut for half second and opened for next half second, at that point LED will be ON just in the main half second. Presently the extent for which the LED is ON over the complete time is known as the Duty Cycle, and can be determined as pursues:

Obligation Cycle =Turn ON schedule/(Turn ON time

+ Turn OFF time)

Obligation Cycle = (0.5/(0.5+0.5)) = half

So the normal yield voltage will be half of the battery voltage.

As we increment the ON and OFF speed to a level we will see the LED being darkened as opposed to being ON and OFF. This is on the grounds that our eyes can't get frequencies higher than 25Hz obviously. Think about 100ms cycle, LED being OFF for 30msec and ON for 70msec. We will have 70% of stable voltage at the yield, so LED will gleam consistently with 70% of power.

Obligation Ratio goes from 0 to 100. '0' signifies totally OFF and '100' being totally ON. This Duty Ratio is significant for the Servo Motor. The situation of Servo Motor is being dictated by this Duty Ratio. Check this for Pulse width Modulation exhibition with Light Emitting Diode as well as Raspberry Pi.

Servo Motor and PWM:

A Servo Motor is a mix of DC engine, position control framework and apparatuses. Servos have numerous applications in the cutting edge world and with that, they are accessible in various shapes and sizes. We will utilize SG90 Servo Motor in this instructional exercise, it is one of the famous and least expensive one. SG90 is a 180 degree servo. So with this servo we can situate the hub from 0-180 degrees.

A Servo Motor for the most part has three wires, one is for positive voltage, another is for ground and last one is for position setting. The Red wire is associated with control, Brown wire is associated with ground and Yellow wire (or WHITE) is associated with signal.

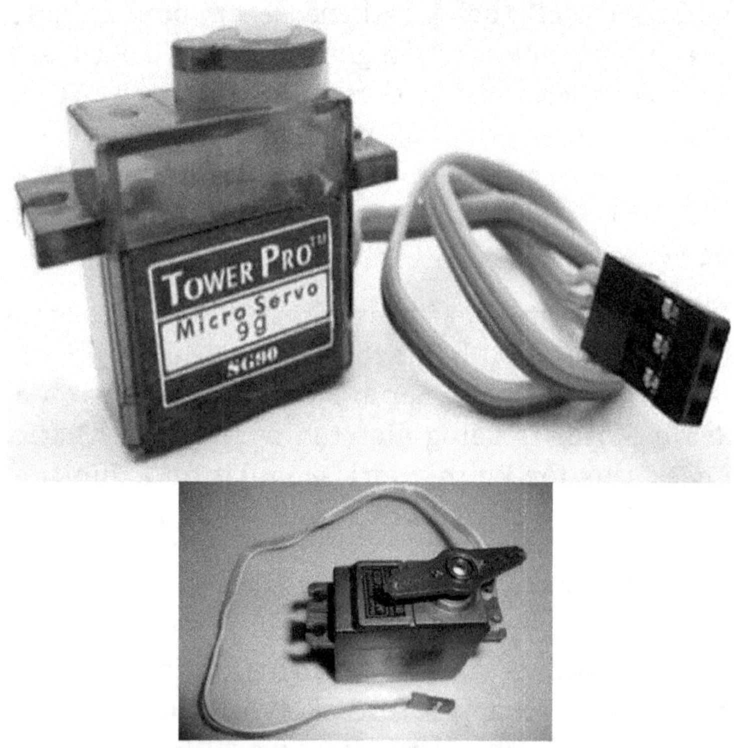

In servo, we have a control framework which takes

the Pulse width Modulation signal from Signal pin. It disentangles the sign and gets the obligation proportion from it. From that point onward, it looks at the proportion to the predefined positions esteems. On the off chance that there is a distinction in the qualities, it alters the situation of the servo as needs be. So the pivot position of the servo engine depends on the obligation proportion of the PWM signal at the Signal pin.

The recurrence of PWM (Pulse Width Modulated) sign can change dependent on sort of servo engine. For SG90 the recurrence of PWM signal is 50Hz. To discover the recurrence of activity for your servo, check the Datasheet for that specific model. So once the recurrence is chosen, the other significant thing here is the DUTY RATIO of the Pulse width Modulation signal.

The table underneath shows the Servo Position for that specific Duty Ratio. You can get any point in the middle of by picking the worth in like manner. So for 45º of servo the Duty Ratio ought to be '5' or 5%.

POSITION	DUTY RATIO
0º	2.5
90º	7.5

180º	12.5

Before Interfacing Servo Motor to Raspberry Pi, you can test your servo with the assistance of this Servo Motor Tester Circuit. Additionally check our beneath Servo ventures:

- Servo Motor Control utilizing Arduino

- Servo Motor Control with Arduino Due

- Servo Motor Interfacing with 8051 Micro-controller

- Servo Motor Control utilizing MATLAB

- Servo Motor Control by Flex Sensor
- Servo Position Control with Weight (Force Sensor)

Components Required:

Here we are utilizing Raspberry Pi 2 Model B with Raspbian Jessie OS. All the essential Hardware and Software prerequisites are recently talked about, you can find it in the Raspberry Pi Introduction, other than that we need:

- Connecting pins
- SG90 Servo Motor

- 1000uF capacitor
- Breadboard

Circuit Diagram:

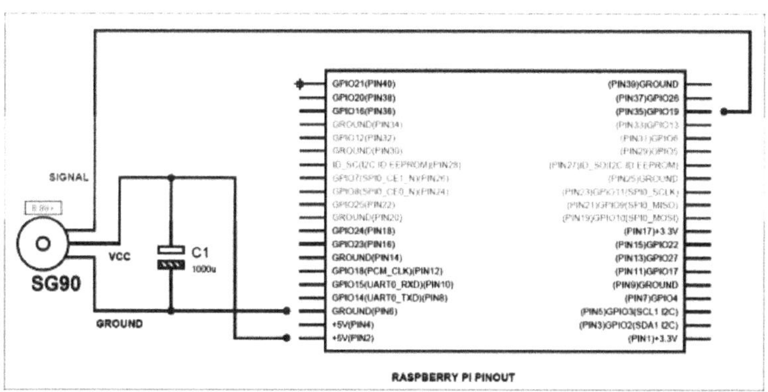

A1000μF must be associated over the +5V control rail generally the PI may close down arbitrarily while controlling the servo.

Working and Programming Explanation:

Once everything is associated according to the circuit chart, we can turn ON the PI to compose the program in PYHTON.

We will discuss barely any directions which we are gonna to use in PYHTON program,

We are gonna to import GPIO document from library, underneath work empowers us to program GPIO pins of PI. We are additionally renaming "GPIO" to "IO", so in the program at whatever point we need to allude to GPIO pins we will utilize the word 'IO'.

```
import RPi.GPIO as IO
```

At times, when the GPIO pins, which we are attempting to utilize, may be doing some different capacities. All things considered, we will get admonitions while executing the program. Beneath order advises the PI to overlook the alerts and continue with the program.

```
IO.setwarnings(False)
```

We can allude the GPIO pins of PI, either by nail number to board otherwise by their capacity number. Like 'PIN 29' on the board is 'GPIO 5'. So we advise here possibly we will speak to the pin here by '29' or '5'.

```
IO.setmode (IO.BCM)
```

We are setting PIN 39 or GPIO 19 as yield pin. We will get PWM yield from this pin.

```
IO.setup(19,IO.OUT)
```

Subsequent to setting the yield pin, we have to arrangement the pin as PWM yield pin,

```
p = IO.PWM(output channel , frequency of PWM signal)
```

The above direction is for setting up the channel and furthermore for setting up the recurrence of the Channel". 'p' here is a variable it very well may be anything. We are utilizing GPIO19 as the PWM "Yield channel. "Recurrence of PWM signal" we will pick 50, as SG90 working recurrence is 50Hz.

Beneath order is utilized to begin PWM signal age. 'DUTYCYCLE' is for setting the 'Turn On' proportion as clarified previously,

```
p.start(DUTYCYCLE)
```

Underneath direction is utilized as everlastingly circle, with this order the announcements inside this circle will be executed ceaselessly.

```
While 1:
```

Here the program for Controlling the Servo utilizing Raspberry Pi gives a PWM signal at GPIO19. The Duty

Ratio of the PWM signal is changed between three qualities for three seconds. So for consistently the Servo pivots to a position dictated by the Duty Ratio. The servo persistently pivots to 0º, 90º and 180º in three seconds.

Code

```
import RPi.GPIO as IO      # calling for header file for
GPIO's of PI
import time                # calling for time to provide
delays in program
IO.setwarnings(False)      # do not show any warnings
IO.setmode (IO.BCM)        # programming the GPIO by
BCM pin numbers. (like PIN29 as'GPIO5')
IO.setup(19,IO.OUT)        # initialize GPIO19 as an
output
p = IO.PWM(19,50)          # GPIO19 as PWM output,
with 50Hz frequency
p.start(7.5)               # generate PWM signal with
7.5% duty cycle
while 1:                               # execute loop
forever
    p.ChangeDutyCycle(7.5)         # change duty cycle
for getting the servo position to 90º
    time.sleep(1)                  # sleep for 1 second
    p.ChangeDutyCycle(12.5)        # change duty cycle
for getting the servo position to 180º
    time.sleep(1)                  # sleep for 1 second
    p.ChangeDutyCycle(2.5)         # change duty cycle
```

for getting the servo position to 0º

```
    time.sleep(1)              # sleep for 1 second
```

3. ROOM TEMPERATURE MEASUREMENT WITH RASPBERRY PI

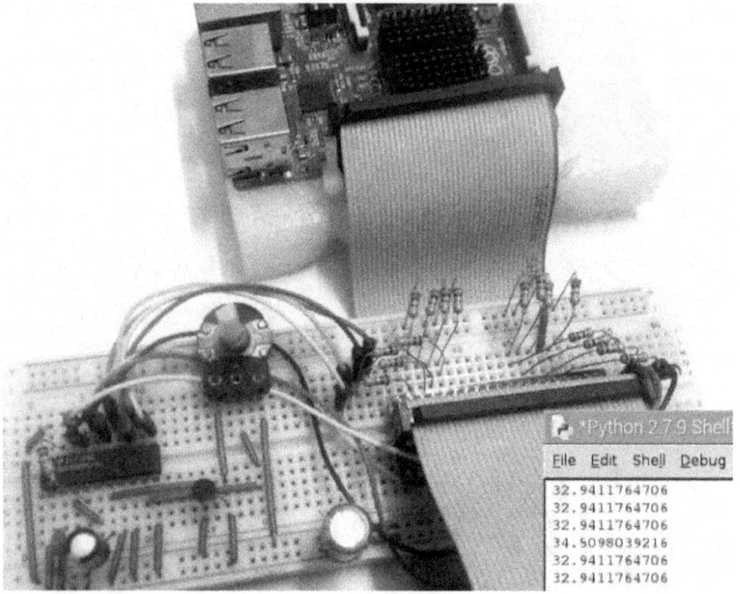

We have generally secured all the Basic Components interfacing with Raspberry Pi in our Raspberry Pi Tutorial Series. We have canvassed every one of the Tutorials in basic and point by point way, so anybody, regardless of whether he has worked with Raspberry Pi or not, can gain from this Series effectively. What's more, as a result of experiencing every one of the instructional exercises you will have the option to construct some High Level activities utilizing Raspberry Pi.

So here we are planning first application dependent

on the past instructional exercises. The principal fundamental application is a Reading Room Temperature by Raspberry Pi. Furthermore, you can screen the Readings on PC.

As talked about in past instructional exercises, there are no Analog-to-Digital Converter diverts given inside in Raspberry Pi. So in the event that we need to interface any simple sensors we require an Analog-to-Digital Converter change unit. What's more, in one of our instructional exercises we have Interfaced ADC0804 chip to Raspberry Pi to peruse a simple worth. So experience it before building this Room Temperature Thermometer.

ADC0804 and Raspberry Pi:

ADC0804 is a chip intended to change over simple sign in to 8 piece advanced information. This chip is one of the well known arrangement of ADC. It's a 8bit change unit, so we have qualities or 0 to 255 qualities. The goals of this chip changes dependent on the reference voltage we pick, we will speak increasingly about it later. The following is the Pinout of ADC0804:

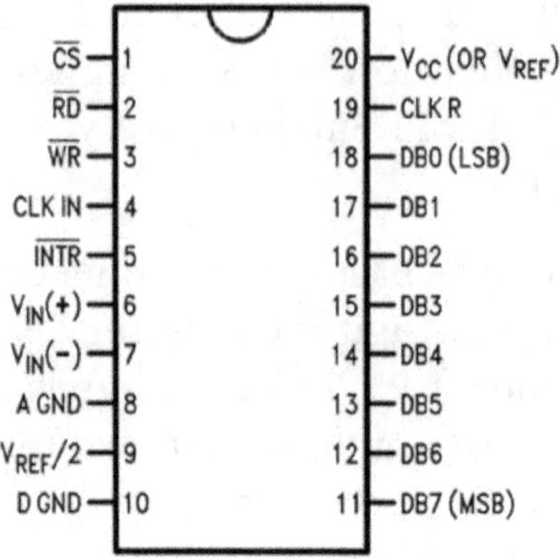

Presently another significant thing here is, the ADC0804 works at 5V thus it gives yield in 5V rationale sign. In 8 pin yield (speaking to 8bits), each pin gives +5V yield to speak to logic'1'. So the issue is the PI rationale is of +3.3v, so you can't give +5V rationale to the +3.3V GPIO pin of PI. On the off chance that you offer +5V to any GPIO pin of PI, the board gets harmed.

So to step-down rationale level from +5V, we will utilize voltage divider circuit. We have talked about Voltage Divider Circuit already investigate it for additional explanation. What we will do is, we utilize two resistors to separate +5V rationale into 2*2.5V rationales. So after division we will give +2.5v rationale to PI. Along these lines, at whatever point rationale '1' is introduced by ADC0804 we will see +2.5V at the PI GPIO Pin, rather than +5V.

LM35 Temperature Sensor:

Presently for Reading Temperature of Room, we require a sensor. Here we are gonna to utilize LM35 Temperature Sensor. Temperature is typically estimated in "Centigrade" or "Fahrenheit". "LM35" sensor gives yield in degree Centigrade.

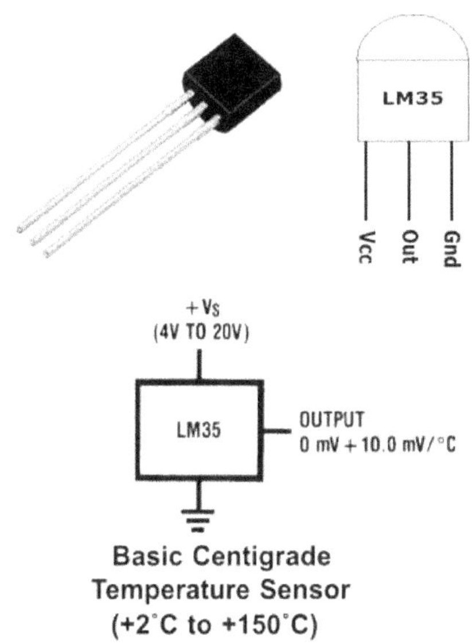

As appeared in figure, LM35 is a 3 pin transistor like gadget. The pins are numbered as,

PIN1 = Vcc - Power (Connected to +5V)

PIN2 = Signal otherwise Output (associated with Analog-to-Digital Converter chip)

PIN3 = Ground (Connected to ground)

This sensor gives variable voltage at the yield, in light of temperature. For each +1 centigrade ascent in temperature there will be +10mV higher voltage at the yield pin. So if the temperature is 0? centigrade the yield of sensor will be 0V, if the temperature is 10? centigrade the yield of sensor will be +100mV, if the temperature is 25? centigrade the yield of sensor will be +250mV.

Components Required:

Here we are utilizing Raspberry Pi two Model B with Raspbian Jessie OS. All the essential Hardware and Software necessities are recently talked about, you can find it in the Raspberry Pi Introduction, other than that we need:

- Connecting pins
- 1K? resistor (17 pieces)
- 10K pot
- 0.1µF capacitor
- 100µF capacitor
- 1000µF capacitor
- ADC0804 IC
- LM35 Temperature Sensor
- Bread Board

Circuit and Working Explanation:

The associations which are accomplished for Connecting Raspberry to ADC0804 and LM35, are appeared in the circuit chart underneath.

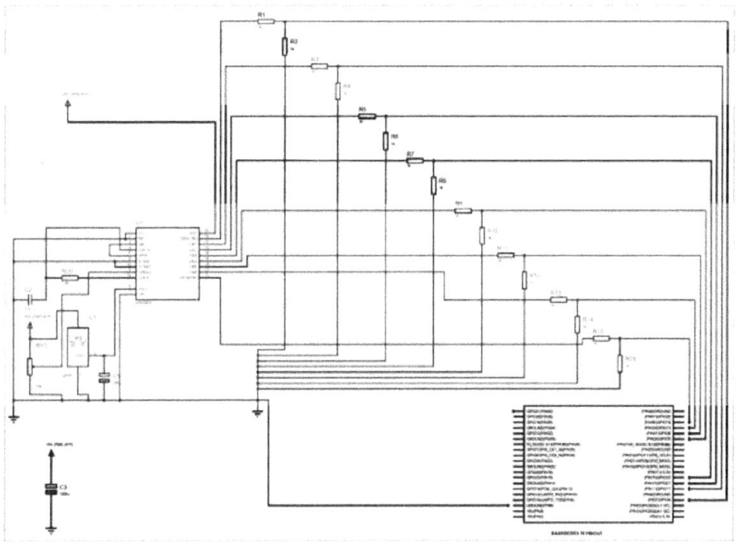

The LM35 yield has part of voltage vacillations; so a 100uF capacitor is utilized to smooth out the yield, as appeared in the figure.

The ADC consistently have loads of commotion, this clamor can enormously influence the exhibition, so we utilize 0.1uF capacitor for Noise Filtration. Without this there will be part of variances at yield.

The chip takes a shot at RC (Resistor-Capacitor) oscillator clock. As appeared in circuit graph, C2 and R20 structure a Clock. The significant thing to recall here is the capacitor C2 can be changed to a lower an incentive for higher pace of ADC transformation. Anyway with higher speed there will be decline in precision. So if the application requires higher precision, pick the capacitor with higher worth and for higher speed pick the capacitor with lower esteem.

As told before the LM35 gives +10mV to each centigrade. The most extreme temperature that can be estimated by the LM35 is 150º centigrade. So we will have a limit of 1.5V at the LM35 yield terminal. Be that as it may, the default reference voltage of ADC0804 is +5V. So on the off chance that we utilize that reference esteem, the goals of the yield will be low since we would utilize a limit of (5/1.5) 34% of advanced yield run.

Fortunately the ADC0804 has a movable Vref pin (PIN9) as demonstrated it its Pin Diagram above. So we will set the Vref of the chip to +2V. To set Vref +2V, we have to give a voltage of +1V (VREF/2) at PIN9. Here we are utilizing 10K pot to alter the voltage at PIN9 to +1V. Utilize the voltmeter to get the precise voltage.

We have recently utilized LM35 Temperature Sensor to Read the Room temperature with Arduino and with AVR Microcontroller. Likewise check Humidity and Temperature Measurement utilizing Arduino

Programming Explanation:

Once everything is associated according to the circuit outline, we can turn ON the PI to compose the program in PYHTON.

We will discuss hardly any directions which we are gonna to use in PYHTON program,

We are gonna to import General Purpose Input Output record from library, beneath
work empowers us to program GPIO pins of PI. We are additionally renaming "GPIO" to "IO", so in the program at whatever point we need to allude to GPIO pins we will utilize the word 'IO'.

```
import RPi.GPIO as IO
```

Now and then, when the GPIO pins, which we are attempting to utilize, may be doing some different capacities. All things considered, we will get alerts while executing the program. Beneath direction advises the PI to overlook the admonitions and continue with the program.

```
IO.setwarnings(False)
```

We can allude the General Purpose Input Output pins of PI, either by nail number to board otherwise by their capacity number. Like 'PIN 29' on the board is 'GPIO 5'. So we advise here it is possible that we will speak to the pin here by '29' or '5'.

```
IO.setmode (IO.BCM)
```

We are setting 8 pins as info pins. We will recognize 8 piece of ADC information by these pins.

```
IO.setup(4,IO.IN)

IO.setup(17,IO.IN)

IO.setup(27,IO.IN)

IO.setup(22,IO.IN)

IO.setup(5,IO.IN)

IO.setup(6,IO.IN)

IO.setup(13,IO.IN)

IO.setup(19,IO.IN)
```

In case the condition in the supports is valid, the announcements inside the circle will be executed once. So on the off chance that the GPIO pin 19 goes high, at that point the announcements inside the IF circle will be executed once. On the off chance that the GPIO pin 19 doesn't goes high, at that point the announcements inside the IF circle won't be executed.

```
if(IO.input(19) == True):
```

Beneath order is utilized as always circle, with this direction the announcements inside this circle will be executed persistently.

```
While 1:
```

Further Explanation of Code is given in Code Section Below.

Subsequent to composing the program it's a great opportunity to execute it. Prior to executing program, lets talks what's going on in the circuit as a Summary. First LM35 sensor recognizes the room temperature and gives a simple voltage at its yield. This variable voltage speaks to the temperature straightly with +10mV per ºC. This sign is encouraged to ADC0804 chip, this chip changes over the Analog incentive to advanced an incentive with 255/200=1.275 tally per10mv or 1.275count for 1degree. This include is taken in by the PI General Purpose Input Output. The program changes over the check to temperature worth and showcases it on the screen. The ordinary temperature read by PI is demonstrated as follows,

Subsequently we this Raspberry Pi temperature screen.

Code

```
#working
import RPi.GPIO as IO          # calling for header file
which helps us use GPIO's of PI
import time                    # calling for time to provide
delays in program
import sys
IO.setwarnings(False)       # do not show any warnings
x = 1
b0 = 0                          # integer for storing the delay
multiple
b1 = 0
b2 = 0
b3 = 0
b4 = 0
b5 = 0
b6 = 0
b7 = 0
IO.setmode (IO.BCM)            # programming the GPIO
by BCM pin numbers. (like PIN29 as'GPIO5')
IO.setup(4,IO.IN)             # initialize GPIO Pins as
input
```

```python
IO.setup(17,IO.IN)
IO.setup(27,IO.IN)
IO.setup(22,IO.IN)
IO.setup(5,IO.IN)
IO.setup(6,IO.IN)
IO.setup(13,IO.IN)
IO.setup(19,IO.IN)
while 1:                      # execute loop forever
  if(IO.input(19) == True):
    time.sleep(0.001)
    if(IO.input(19) == True):
      b7=1                    # if pin19 is high bit 7 is true
  if(IO.input(13) == True):
    time.sleep(0.001)
    if(IO.input(13) == True):
      b6=1                    # if pin13 is high bit 6 is true
  if(IO.input(6) == True):
    time.sleep(0.001)
    if(IO.input(6) == True):
      b5=1                    # if pin6 is high bit 5 is true
  if(IO.input(5) == True):
    time.sleep(0.001)
    if(IO.input(5) == True):
      b4=1                    # if pin5 is high bit 4 is true
  if(IO.input(22) == True):
    time.sleep(0.001)
    if(IO.input(22) == True):
      b3=1                    # if pin22 is high bit 3 is true
  if(IO.input(27) == True):
    time.sleep(0.001)
```

```python
    if(IO.input(27) == True):
      b2=1                       # if pin27 is high bit2 is true
    if(IO.input(17) == True):
      time.sleep(0.001)
      if(IO.input(17) == True):
        b1=1                     # if pin17 is high bit1 is true
    if(IO.input(4) == True):
      time.sleep(0.001)
      if(IO.input(4) == True):
        b0=1                     # if pin4 is high bit0 is true


    x = (1*b0)+(2*b1)                  # representing the bit
values from LSB to MSB
    x = x+(4*b2)+(8*b3)
    x = x+(16*b4)+(32*b5)
    x = x+(64*b6)+(128*b7)
    x = x/1.275


#temp=100,ref=2000mv,read=255/200=1.275count
per10mv or 1.275count for 1degree

    print(x)                     # print the ADC value
    b0=b1=b2=b3=b4=b5=b6=b7=0    # reset the values
    time.sleep(0.01)             # wait for 10ms
```

4. CAPACITIVE TOUCH PAD WITH RASPBERRY PI

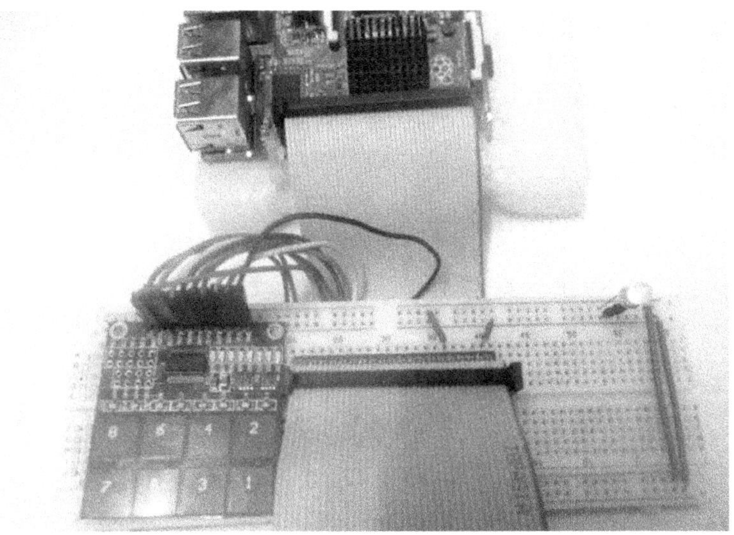

Raspberry Pi is an ARM engineering processor based board intended for electronic designers and specialists. The PI is one of most confided in venture improvement stages out there now. With higher processor speed and 1 GB RAM, the PI can be used for some, prominent ventures like Image preparing and Internet of Things.

For doing any of prominent tasks, one have to comprehend the essential elements of PI. We will cover all the fundamental functionalities of Raspberry Pi in

these instructional exercises. In every instructional exercise we will examine one of elements of PI. Before the finish of this Raspberry Pi Tutorial Series, you will have the option to do prominent tasks independent from anyone else. Experience
instructional exercises:

- Beginning with Raspberry Pi

- Raspberry Pi Configuration

- Driven Blinky

- Raspberry Pi Button Interfacing

- Raspberry Pi PWM age

- Controlling DC Motor utilizing Raspberry Pi

- Stepper Motor Control with Raspberry Pi
- Interfacing Shift Register with Raspberry Pi

In this instructional exercise, we will Interface a Capacitive Touchpad to Raspberry Pi. Capacitive Touchpad has eight keys from one to eight. These keys are not actually keys, they are Touch Sensitive Pads set on the PCB. At the point when we contact one of the cushions, the cushions experience the difference in capacitance on its surface. This change is caught by the control unit and control unit, as a reaction, pulls a relating pin high at the yield side.

We will connect this Capacitive Touchpad Sensor Module to the Raspberry Pi, to utilize it as information gadget for the PI.

We will examine somewhat about Raspberry Pi General Purpose Input/Output Pins before going any further.

GPIO Pins:

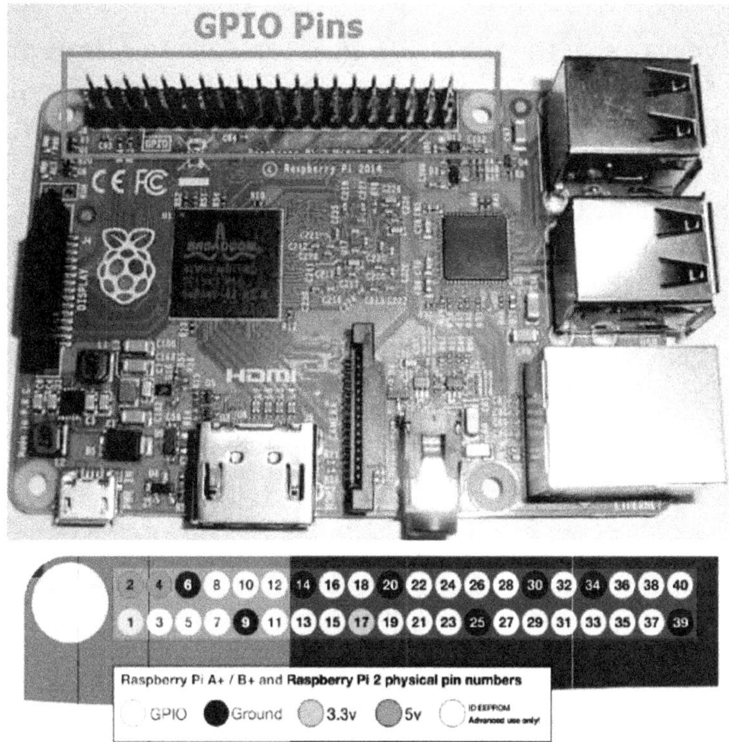

As appeared in above figure, there are 40output pins for the PI. In any case, when you take a gander at the second figure underneath, you can see not every one of the 40 pin out can be modified to our utilization.

These are just 26 GPIO pins which can be modified. These pins go from GPIO2 to GPIO27.

These 26 GPIO pins can be customized according to require. A portion of these pins additionally play out some extraordinary capacities, we will examine about that later. With unique GPIO set aside, we have 17 GPIO staying (Light green Color).

Every one of these 17 GPIO pins can convey a limit of 15mA current. What's more, the total of flows from all GPIO can't surpass 50mA. So we can attract a limit of 3mA normal from every one of these GPIO pins. So one ought not mess with these things except if you recognize what you are doing.

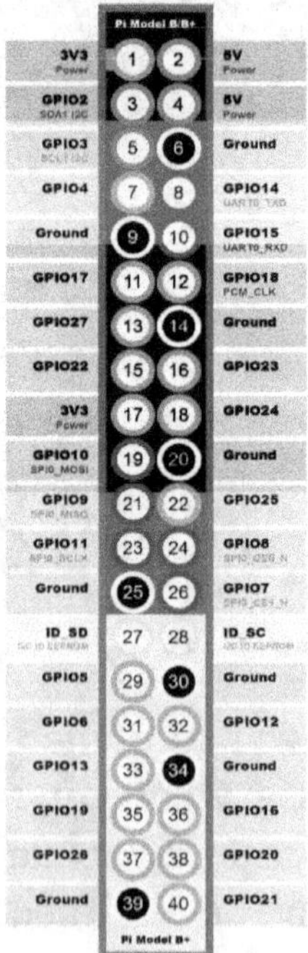

Presently another significant thing here is that, PI rationale control is of +3.3v, so you can't give more than +3.3V rationale to GPIO pin of PI. In the event that you offer +5V to any GPIO pin of PI, the board gets harmed. So we have to control the Capacitive Touchpad by +3.3V, for getting appropriate rationale yields for PI.

Components Required:

Here we are utilizing Raspberry Pi 2 Model B with Raspbian Jessie OS. All the fundamental Hardware and Software prerequisites are recently examined, you can find it in the Raspberry Pi Introduction, other than that we need:

- Associating pins

- Capacitive Touch Pad

Circuit Diagram:

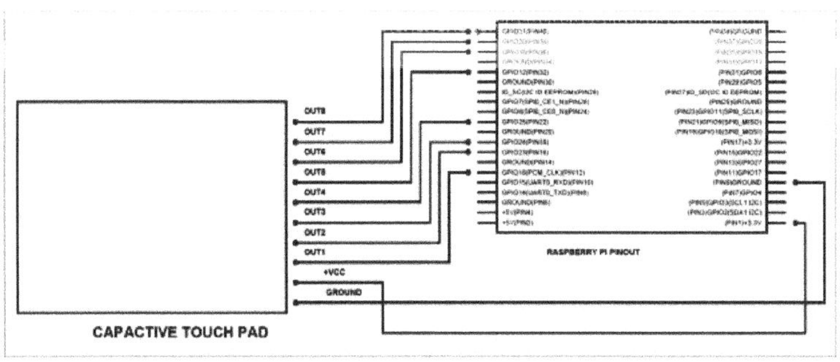

The associations, which are accomplished for Capacitive Touchpad Interfacing, are appeared in the circuit graph above.

Working and Programming Explanation:

Once everything is associated according to the circuit graph, we can turn ON the PI to compose the program in PYHTON.

We will discuss not many directions which we are gonna to use in PYHTON program,

We are gonna to import GPIO document from library, underneath work empowers us to program GPIO pins of PI. We are likewise renaming "GPIO" to "IO", so in the program at whatever point we need to allude to GPIO pins we will utilize the word 'IO'.

```
import RPi.GPIO as IO
```

Now and again, when the GPIO pins, which we are attempting to utilize, may be doing some different capacities. All things considered, we will get admonitions while executing the program. Underneath order advises the PI to disregard the alerts and continue with the program.

```
IO.setwarnings(False)
```

We can allude the General Purpose Input/Output pins of PI, either by nail number to board otherwise by their capacity number. Like 'PIN 29' on the board is 'GPIO5'. So we advise here possibly we will speak to the pin here by '29' or '5'.

```
IO.setmode (IO.BCM)
```

We are setting 8 pins as information pins. We will identify 8 key yields from Capacitive Touchpad.

```
IO.setup(21,IO.IN)

IO.setup(20,IO.IN)

IO.setup(16,IO.IN)

IO.setup(12,IO.IN)

IO.setup(25,IO.IN)

IO.setup(24,IO.IN)

IO.setup(23,IO.IN)
```

```
IO.setup(18,IO.IN)
```

In case the condition in the props is valid, the announcements inside the circle will be executed once. So in the event that the GPIO pin 21 goes high, at that point the announcements inside the IF circle will be executed once. In the event that the GPIO pin 21 doesn't goes high, at that point the announcements inside the IF circle won't be executed.

```
if(IO.input(21) == True):
```

Beneath direction is utilized as perpetually circle, with this order the announcements inside this circle will be executed ceaselessly.

```
While 1:
```

When we compose the underneath program in PYTHON and execute it we are all set. At the point when the cushion is contacted, the module pulls up the relating pin and this trigger is distinguished by the PI. After the identification, the PI prints the fitting key on the screen.

Henceforth we have Interfaced Capacitive Touchpad to PI.

Code

```python
import RPi.GPIO as IO          # calling for header file for GPIO's of PI
import time                    # calling for time to provide delays in program
IO.setwarnings(False)          # do not show any warnings
IO.setmode (IO.BCM)            # programming the GPIO by BCM pin numbers. (like PIN29 as 'GPIO5')
IO.setup(21,IO.IN)             # initialize GPIO Pins as an Input.
IO.setup(20,IO.IN)
IO.setup(16,IO.IN)
IO.setup(12,IO.IN)
IO.setup(25,IO.IN)
IO.setup(24,IO.IN)
IO.setup(23,IO.IN)
IO.setup(18,IO.IN)

while 1:
  if(IO.input(21) == True):
    time.sleep(0.001)
    if(IO.input(21) == True):
      print (8)                # if PIN21 is high print '8'
  if(IO.input(20) == True):
    time.sleep(0.001)
    if(IO.input(20) == True):
      print (7)                # if PIN20 is high print '7'
  if(IO.input(16) == True):
    time.sleep(0.001)
```

```python
    if(IO.input(16) == True):
      print (6)                    # if PIN16 is high print'6'
  if(IO.input(12) == True):
    time.sleep(0.001)
    if(IO.input(12) == True):
      print (5)                    # if PIN12 is high print'5'
  if(IO.input(25) == True):
    time.sleep(0.001)
    if(IO.input(25) == True):
      print (4)                    # if PIN25 is high print'4'
  if(IO.input(24) == True):
    time.sleep(0.001)
    if(IO.input(24) == True):
      print (3)                    # if PIN24 is high print'3'
  if(IO.input(23) == True):
    time.sleep(0.001)
    if(IO.input(23) == True):
      print (2)                    # if PIN23 is high print'2'
  if(IO.input(18) == True):
    time.sleep(0.001)
    if(IO.input(18) == True):
      print (1)                    # if PIN18 is high print'1'
time.sleep(0.2)                    # wait for 200ms
```

5. RASPBERRY PI ADC TUTORIAL

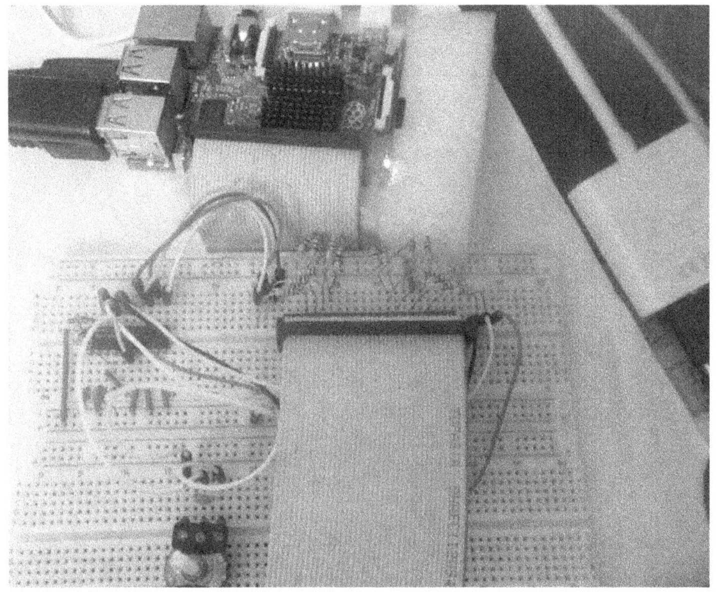

Raspberry Pi is an ARM engineering processor based board intended for electronic specialists and specialists. The PI is one of most confided in venture improvement stages out there now. With higher processor speed and 1 GB RAM, the PI can be utilized for some, prominent tasks like Image handling as well as Internet of Things.

For doing any of prominent activities, one have to comprehend the essential elements of PI. We will cover all the fundamental functionalities of Raspberry Pi in these instructional exercises. In every instructional exercise we will talk about one of elements of PI. Before the finish of this Raspberry Pi Tutorial Series, you will have the option to do prominent tasks without anyone else's input. Experience beneath instructional exercises:

- Beginning with Raspberry Pi

- Raspberry Pi Configuration

- Driven Blinky

- Raspberry Pi Button Interfacing

- Raspberry Pi PWM age

- Controlling DC Motor utilizing Raspberry Pi

- Stepper Motor Control with Raspberry Pi

- Interfacing Shift Register with Raspberry Pi

In this instructional exercise, we will Interface an (Analog to Digital Conversion) chip to Raspberry Pi. We know every parameters of simple, implies there shift persistently after some time. State for an occurrence temperature of the room, the room temperature changes with time constantly. This temperature is furnished with decimal numbers. Be that as it may, in advanced world, there are no decimal numbers, so we have to change over the Analog incentive to Digital worth. This change procedure is finished by ADC system. Get familiar with ADC here: Introduction to ADC0804

ADC0804 and Raspberry Pi:

Ordinary controllers have ADC channels yet for PI there are no ADC channels given inside. So on the off chance that we need to interface any simple sensors we need an ADC change unit. So for that reasons we are gonna to Interface ADC0804 with Raspberry Pi.

ADC0804 is a chip intended to change over simple sign into 8 piece advanced information. This chip is one of the well known arrangement of ADC. It's a 8bit change unit, so we have qualities or 0 to 255 qualities. With an estimating voltage of most extreme 5V, we will have a change for each 19.5mV. The following is the Pinout of ADC0804:

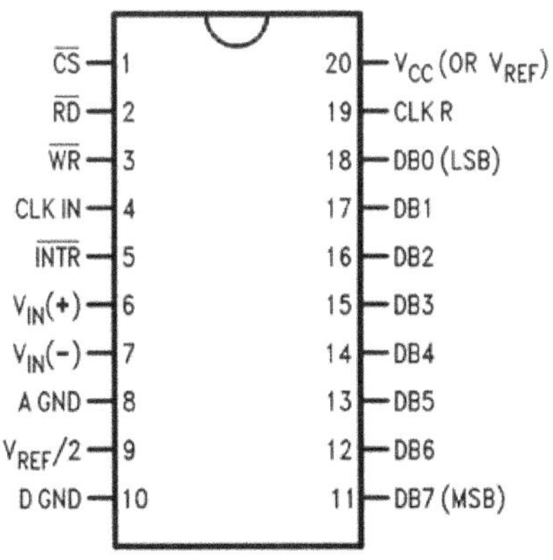

Presently another significant thing here is, the ADC0804 works at 5V thus it gives yield in 5V rationale sign. In 8 pin yield (speaking to 8bits), each pin gives +5V yield to speak to logic'1'. So the issue is the PI rationale is of +3.3v, so you can't give +5V rationale to the +3.3V GPIO pin of PI. In the event that you offer +5V to any GPIO pin of PI, the board gets harmed.

So to step-down rationale level from +5V, we will utilize voltage divider circuit. We have talked about Voltage Divider Circuit already investigate it for additional explanation. What we will do is, we utilize two resistors to separate +5V rationale into 2*2.5V rationales. So after division we will give +2.5v rationale to PI. In this way, at whatever point rationale '1' is introduced by ADC0804 we will see +2.5V at the PI GPIO Pin, rather than +5V.

Get familiar with GPIO Pins of Raspberry Pi here and experience our past instructional exercises.

Components Required:

Here we are utilizing Raspberry Pi two Model B with Raspbian Jessie OS. All the essential Hardware and Software necessities are recently talked about, you can find it in the Raspberry Pi Introduction, other than that we need:

- Connecting pins
- 220? or 1K?resistor (17 pieces)
- 10K pot
- ADC0804 IC
- 0.1µF capacitor (two pieces)
- Bread Board

Circuit Explanation:

It chips away at supply voltage of +5v as well as can quantify a variable voltage go in 0-5V territory.

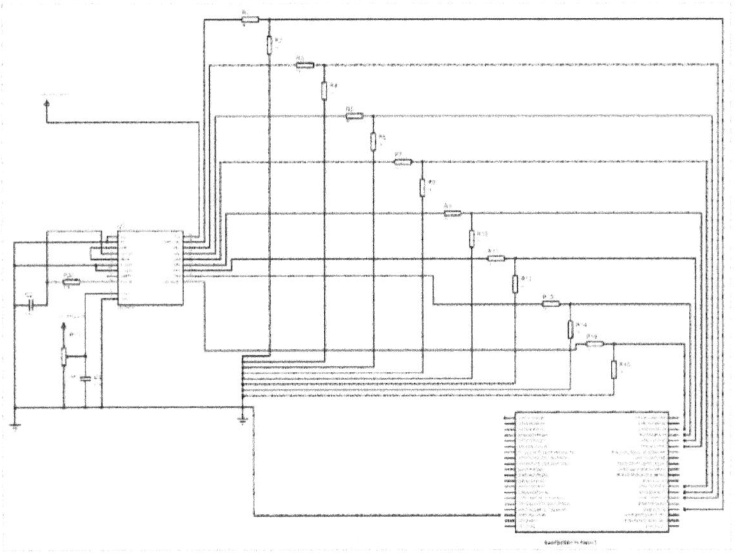

The associations for interfacing ADC0804 to Raspberry PI, are appeared in the circuit graph above.
The ADC consistently have loads of commotion, this

clamor can extraordinarily influence the exhibition, so we utilize 0.1uF capacitor for Noise Filtration. Without this there will be parcel of changes at yield.

The chip deals with RC (Resistor-Capacitor) oscillator clock. As appeared in circuit outline, C2 and R20 structure a Clock. The significant thing to recollect here is the capacitor C2 can be changed to a lower an incentive for higher pace of ADC transformation. Anyway with higher speed there will be decline in precision. So if the application requires higher precision, pick the capacitor with higher worth and for higher speed pick the capacitor with lower esteem.

Programming Explanation:

Once everything is associated according to the circuit outline, we can turn ON the PI to compose the program in PYHTON.

We will discuss barely any directions which we are gonna to use in PYHTON program,

We are gonna to import GPIO record from library, underneath work empowers us to program GPIO pins of PI. We are likewise renaming "GPIO" to "IO", so in the program at whatever point we need to allude to GPIO pins we will utilize the word 'IO'.

```
import RPi.GPIO as IO
```

Some of the time, when the GPIO pins, which we are attempting to utilize, may be doing some different capacities. All things considered, we will get admonitions while executing the program. Underneath order advises the PI to overlook the admonitions and continue with the program.

```
IO.setwarnings(False)
```

We can allude the General Purpose Input Output pins of PI, either by nail number to board otherwise by their capacity number. Like 'PIN 29' on the board is 'GPIO5'. So we advise here it is possible that we will speak to the pin here by '29' or '5'.

```
IO.setmode (IO.BCM)
```

We are setting 8 pins as info pins. We will recognize 8 piece of ADC information by these pins.

```
IO.setup(4,IO.IN)

IO.setup(17,IO.IN)

IO.setup(27,IO.IN)
```

```
IO.setup(22,IO.IN)

IO.setup(5,IO.IN)

IO.setup(6,IO.IN)

IO.setup(13,IO.IN)

IO.setup(19,IO.IN)
```

On the off chance that the condition in the supports is valid, the announcements inside the circle will be implemented once. So on the off chance that the GPIO pin 19 goes high, at that point the announcements inside the IF circle will be executed once. On the off chance that the GPIO pin 19 doesn't goes high, at that point the announcements inside the IF circle won't be executed.

```
if(IO.input(19) == True):
```

Beneath order is utilized as always circle, with this direction the announcements inside this circle will be executed persistently.

```
While 1:
```

Further clarification of Program is given in Code Section Below.

Working:

Subsequent to composing the program and executing it you will see '0'on the screen. '0'means 0 volts at input.

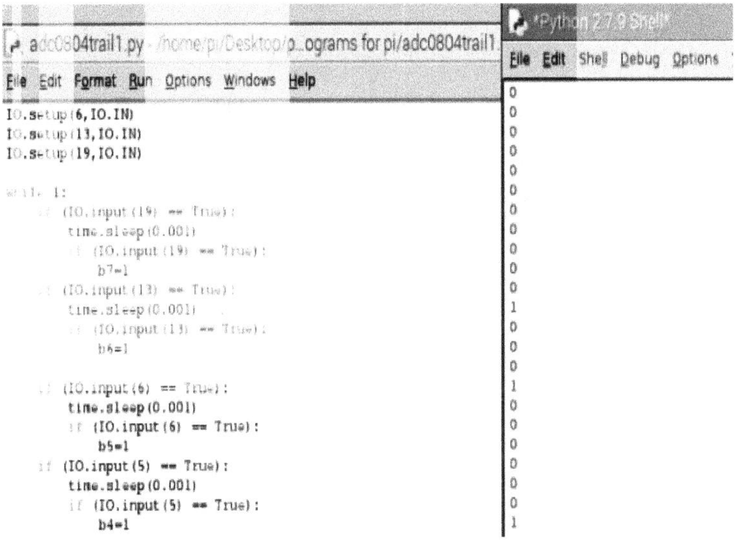

```
adc0804trail1.py - /home/pi/Desktop/p...ograms for pi/adc0804trail1
File  Edit  Format  Run  Options  Windows  Help
IO.setup(6,IO.IN)
IO.setup(13,IO.IN)
IO.setup(19,IO.IN)

while 1:
    if (IO.input(19) == True):
        time.sleep(0.001)
        if (IO.input(19) == True):
            b7=1
    if (IO.input(13) == True):
        time.sleep(0.001)
        if (IO.input(13) == True):
            b6=1

    if (IO.input(6) == True):
        time.sleep(0.001)
        if (IO.input(6) == True):
            b5=1
    if (IO.input(5) == True):
        time.sleep(0.001)
        if (IO.input(5) == True):
            b4=1
```

```
Python 2.7.9 Shell
File  Edit  Shell  Debug  Options
0
0
0
0
0
0
0
0
0
0
0
1
0
0
0
1
0
0
0
0
0
0
1
```

c

In the event that we alter the 10K pot associated with the chip, we will see the adjustment in the qualities on the screen. The qualities on the screen continue looking over persistently, these are the advanced qualities perused by PI.

State on the off chance that we get the pot to the midpoint, we have +2.5V at the ADC0804 input. So we consider 128 to be the screen as demonstrated as follows.

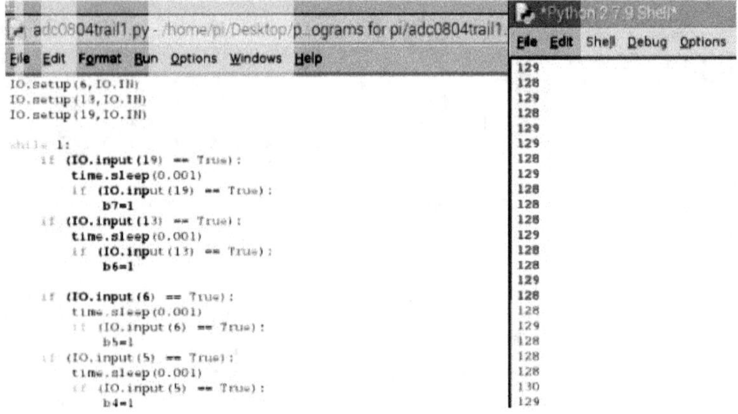

For +5V simple worth, we will have 255.

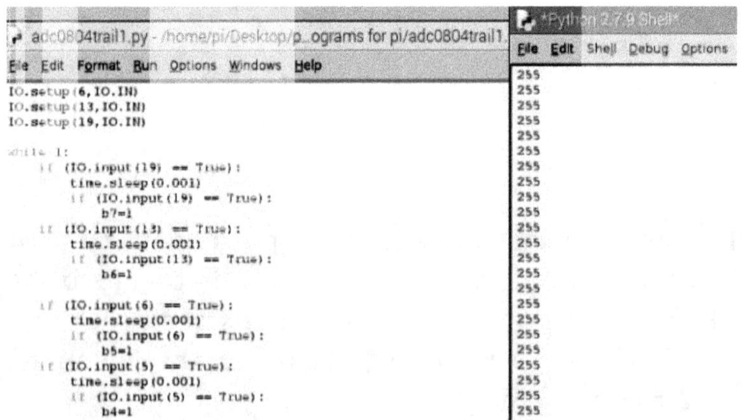

Along these lines, by changing the pot we shift the voltage from 0 to +5V at the ADC0804 input. With this PI read esteems from 0-255. The qualities are imprinted on the screen.

So we have Interfaced ADC0804 to Raspberry Pi.

Code

```
import RPi.GPIO as IO       # calling for header file
which helps us use GPIO's of PI
import time                 # calling for time to provide
delays in program
IO.setwarnings(False)       # do not show any warnings
x = 1
b0 =0                       # integers for storing 8 bits
b1 =0
b2 =0
b3 =0
b4 =0
b5 =0
b6 =0
b7 =0
IO.setmode (IO.BCM)         # programming the GPIO by
BCM pin numbers. (like PIN29 as'GPIO5')
IO.setup(4,IO.IN)           # initialize GPIO Pins as input
IO.setup(17,IO.IN)
IO.setup(27,IO.IN)
IO.setup(22,IO.IN)
```

```python
IO.setup(5,IO.IN)
IO.setup(6,IO.IN)
IO.setup(13,IO.IN)
IO.setup(19,IO.IN)
while 1:                        # execute loop forever
  if(IO.input(19) == True):
    time.sleep(0.001)
    if(IO.input(19) == True):
      b7=1                      # if pin19 is high bit7 is true

  if(IO.input(13) == True):
    time.sleep(0.001)
    if(IO.input(13) == True):
      b6=1                      # if pin13 is high bit6 is true

  if(IO.input(6) == True):
    time.sleep(0.001)
    if(IO.input(6) == True):
      b5=1                      # if pin6 is high bit5 is true

  if(IO.input(5) == True):
    time.sleep(0.001)
    if(IO.input(5) == True):
      b4=1                      # if pin5 is high bit4 is true

  if(IO.input(22) == True):
    time.sleep(0.001)
    if(IO.input(22) == True):
      b3=1                      # if pin22 is high bit3 is true

  if(IO.input(27) == True):
    time.sleep(0.001)
    if(IO.input(27) == True):
```

```python
     b2=1                    # if pin27 is high bit2 is true


if(IO.input(17) == True):
  time.sleep(0.001)
  if(IO.input(17) == True):
    b1=1                    # if pin17 is high bit1 is true

if(IO.input(4) == True):
  time.sleep(0.001)
  if(IO.input(4) == True):
    b0=1                    # if pin4 is high bit0 is true


  x = (1*b0)+(2*b1)
x = x+(4*b2)+(8*b3)
x = x+(16*b4)+(32*b5)
x = x+(64*b6)+(128*b7)              # representing the bit
values from LSB to MSB
print (x)                       # print the ADC value
b0=b1=b2=b3=b4=b5=b6=b7=0    # reset values
time.sleep(0.01)                 # wait for 10ms
```

6. INTERFACING 74HC595 SERIAL SHIFT REGISTER WITH RASPBERRY PI

Raspberry Pi is an ARM design processor based board intended for electronic specialists and specialists. The PI is one of most confided in venture advancement stages out there now. With higher processor speed and 1 GB RAM, the PI can be utilized for some, prominent tasks like Image handling as well as Internet of Things.

For doing any of prominent tasks, one have to comprehend the essential elements of PI. We will cover all the fundamental functionalities of Raspberry Pi in these instructional exercises. In every instructional exercise we will talk about one of elements of PI. Before the finish of this Raspberry Pi Tutorial Series, you will have the option to do prominent undertakings without anyone else's input. Experience beneath instructional exercises:

- Beginning with Raspberry Pi

- Raspberry Pi Configuration

- Driven Blinky

- Raspberry Pi Button Interfacing

- Raspberry Pi PWM age

- Controlling DC Motor utilizing Raspberry Pi

- Stepper Motor Control with Raspberry Pi

In this Raspberry Pi move register instructional exercise, we will Interface Shift Register with Pi. PI has 26 GPIO pins, however when we do ventures like 3D printer, the yield pins gave by PI are insufficient. So we require more yield pins, for adding more yield pins to PI, we include Shift Register Chip. A Shift Register chip takes information from PI board sequentially and gives parallel yield. The chip is of 8bit, so the chip takes 8bits from PI sequentially and afterward gives the 8bit rationale yield through 8 yield pins.

For 8 piece move register, we are going to utilize IC 74HC595. It's a 16 PIN chip. The pin setup of the chip is clarified later beneath in this instructional exercise.

In this instructional exercise, we will utilize three PI's GPIO pins to get eight yields from Shift Register Chip. Recollect here the PINS of chip are for yield just, so we can't interface any sensors to chip yield and anticipate that the PI should understand them. LEDs are associated at the chip yield to see the 8 piece information sent from PI.

We will examine somewhat about Raspberry Pi GPIO Pins before going any further,

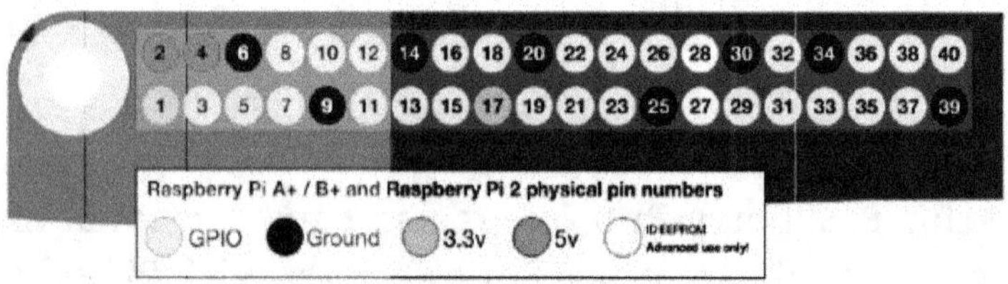

There are 40 GPIO yield sticks in Raspberry Pi 2. Yet, out of 40, just 26 GPIO pins (GPIO2 to GPIO27) can be customized. A portion of these pins play out some extraordinary capacities. With uncommon GPIO set aside, we have just 17 GPIO remaining. Every one of

these 17 GPIO pin can convey a limit of 15mA current. Furthermore, the whole of flows from all GPIO Pins can't surpass 50mA. To find out about GPIO pins, experience: LED Blinking with Raspberry Pi

Components Required:

Here we are utilizing Raspberry Pi two Model B with Raspbian Jessie OS. All the essential Hardware and Software prerequisites are recently examined, you can find it in the Raspberry Pi Introduction, other than that we need:

- Connecting pins
- LED (8)
- 220? or 1K? resistor (6)
- 74HC595 IC
- 0.01μF capacitor
- Bread Board

Circuit Diagram:

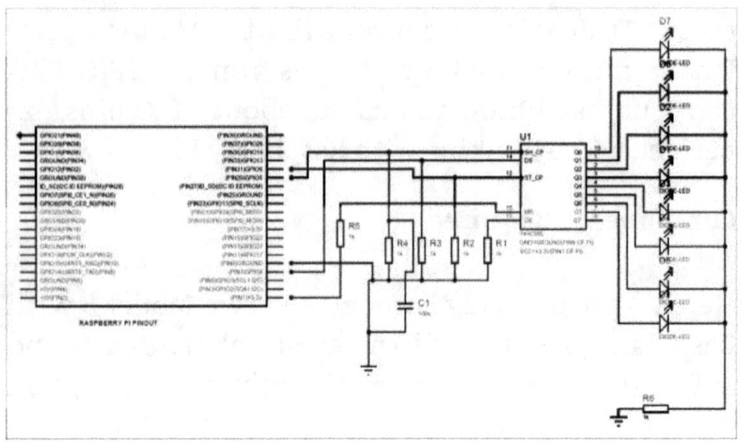

Shift Register IC 74HC595:

How about we talk about the PINS of SHIFT REGISTER we are going to use in here.

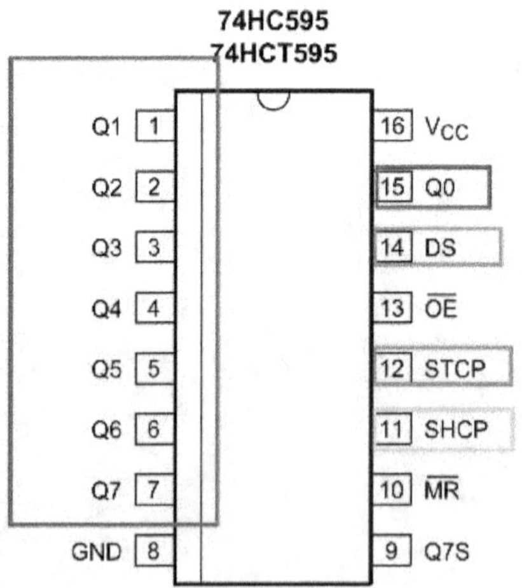

Pin Name	Description
Q0 - Q7	They are the output pins (red rectangle), where we get 8 Bit Data parallel. We will connect eight LED to them to see the parallel output.
Data Pin (DS)	First data is sent bit by bit to this pin. To send 1, we pull-up the DATA pin high and to send 0 we will pull down DATA pin.
Clock Pin (SHCP)	Every pulse at this pin forces the registers to take in one bit of data from DATA pin and store it.
Shift Output (STCP)	After receiving 8 bits, we provide pulse this pin to see the output.

Flow of Working:

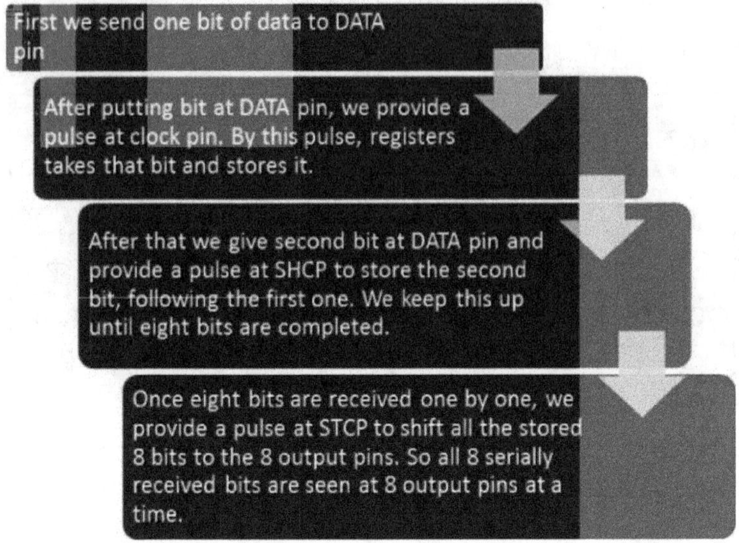

We will pursue the Flow Chart and compose a decimal counter program in PYTHON. At the point when we run the program, we view Light Emitting Diode Counting utilizing Shift Register in Raspberry Pi.

Programming explanation:

Once everything is associated according to the circuit chart, we can turn ON the PI to compose the program in PYHTON.

We will discuss not many directions which we are going to use in PYHTON program,

We are going to import GPIO record from library, beneath work empowers us to program GPIO pins of PI. We are likewise renaming "GPIO" to "IO", so in the program at whatever point we need to allude to GPIO pins we will utilize the word 'IO'.

```
import RPi.GPIO as IO
```

Now and again, when the GPIO pins, which we are attempting to utilize, may be doing some different capacities. All things considered, we will get admonitions while executing the program. Underneath order advises the PI to disregard the admonitions and continue with the program.

```
IO.setwarnings(False)
```

We can allude the General Purpose Input Output pins of PI, either by nail number to board otherwise by their capacity number. Like 'PIN 29' on the board is 'GPIO 5'. So we advise here it is possible that we will speak to the pin here by '29' or '5'.

```
IO.setmode (IO.BCM)
```

We are setting GPIO4, GPIO5 and GPIO6 sticks as yield

```
IO.setup(4,IO.OUT)

IO.setup(5,IO.OUT)

IO.setup(6,IO.OUT)
```

This order executes the circle multiple times.

```
for y in range(8):
```

While 1: is utilized for unendingness circle. With this direction the announcements inside this circle will be executed constantly.

Further clarification of Program is given in Code Section Below. We have all directions expected to send information to the SHIFT REGISTER now.

Code

```
import RPi.GPIO as IO        # calling for header file
which helps us use GPIO's of PI
import time                  # calling for time to provide
delays in program
IO.setwarnings(False)        # do not show any warnings
x=1
IO.setmode (IO.BCM)          # programming the GPIO by
```

```python
BCM pin numbers. (like PIN29 as'GPIO 5')
IO.setup(4,IO.OUT)          # initialize GPIO Pins as an
output.
IO.setup(5,IO.OUT)
IO.setup(6,IO.OUT)
while 1:                    # execute loop forever
  for y in range(8):        # loop for counting up 8 times
    IO.output(4,1)          # pull up the data pin for every
bit.
    time.sleep(0.1)         # wait for 100ms
    IO.output(5,1)          # pull CLOCK pin high
    time.sleep(0.1)
    IO.output(5,0)          # pull CLOCK pin down, to send
a rising edge
    IO.output(4,0)          # clear the DATA pin
    IO.output(6,1)          # pull the SHIFT pin high to put
the 8 bit data out parallel
    time.sleep(0.1)
    IO.output(6,0)          # pull down the SHIFT pin

  for y in range(8):        # loop for counting up 8 times
    IO.output(4,0)          # clear the DATA pin, to send 0
    time.sleep(0.1)         # wait for 100ms
    IO.output(5,1)          # pull CLOCK pin high
    time.sleep(0.1)
    IO.output(5,0)          # pull CLOCK pin down, to send
a rising edge
    IO.output(4,0)          # keep the DATA bit low to keep
the countdown
    IO.output(6,1)          # pull the SHIFT pin high to put
the 8 bit data out parallel
```

```
    time.sleep(0.1)
    IO.output(6,0)
```

time.sleep(0.1)
IO.output(6,0)

7. STEPPER MOTOR CONTROL WITH RASPBERRY PI

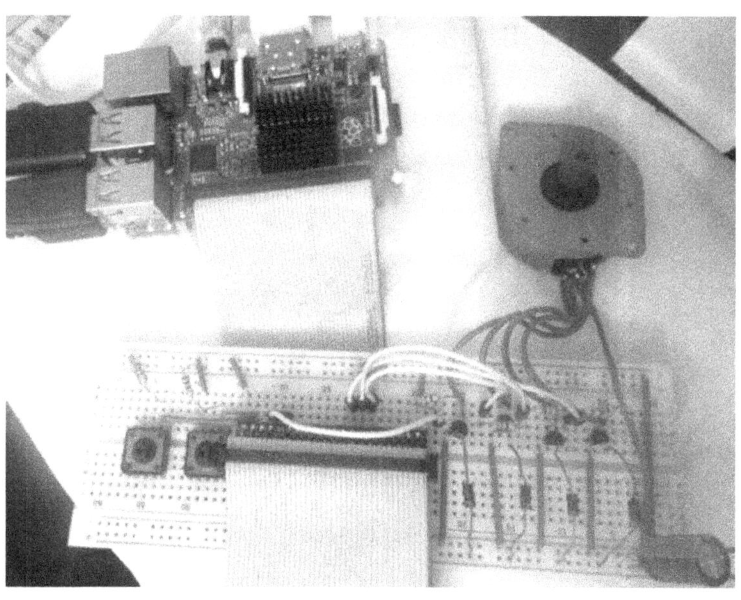

Raspberry Pi is an ARM engineering processor based board intended for electronic designers and specialists. The PI is one of most confided in venture advancement stages out there now. With higher processor speed and 1 GB RAM, the PI can be utilized for some, prominent undertakings like Image handling and Internet of Things.

For doing any of prominent tasks, one have to comprehend the essential elements of PI. We will cover all the fundamental functionalities of Raspberry Pi in these instructional exercises. In every instructional exercise we will talk about one of elements of PI. Before the finish of this Raspberry Pi Tutorial Series, you will have the option to do prominent tasks without anyone else. Experience underneath instructional exercises:

- Beginning with Raspberry Pi

- Raspberry Pi Configuration

- Driven Blinky

- Raspberry Pi Button Interfacing

- Raspberry Pi PWM age

- Controlling DC Motor utilizing Raspberry Pi

In this instructional exercise, we will Control the Speed of a Stepper Motor utilizing Raspberry Pi. In Stepper Motor, as the name itself says, the turn of shaft is in Step structure. There are various kinds of Stepper Motor; in here we will utilize the most mainstream one that is Unipolar Stepper Motor. Not at all like DC engine, we can turn stepper engine to a specific edge by giving it appropriate directions.

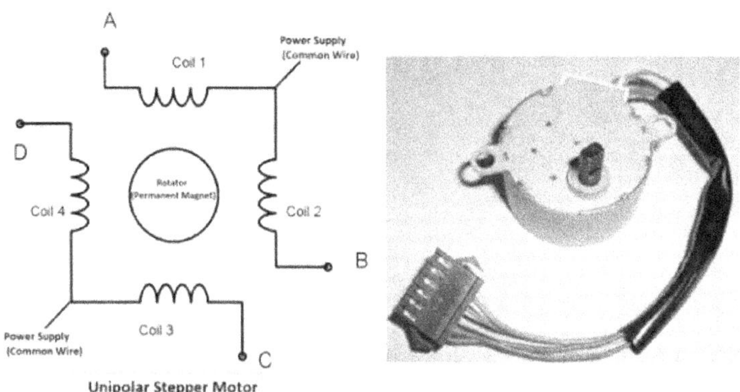

Unipolar Stepper Motor

To turn this Four Stage Stepper Motor, we will convey control beats by utilizing Stepper Motor Driver Circuit. The driver circuit takes rationale triggers from PI. In the event that we control the rationale triggers, we control the power beats and henceforth the speed of stepper engine.

There are 40 General Purpose Input Output yield sticks in Raspberry Pi 2. Be that as it may, out of 40, just 26 General Purpose Input Output pins (General Purpose Input Output 2 to General Purpose Input Output 27) can be customized. A portion of these pins play out some uncommon capacities. With extraordinary GPIO set aside, we have just 17 GPIO remaining. Every one of these 17 GPIO pin can convey a limit of 15mA current. Furthermore, the aggregate of flows from all GPIO Pins can't surpass 50mA. To find out about GPIO pins, experience: LED Blinking with Raspberry Pi

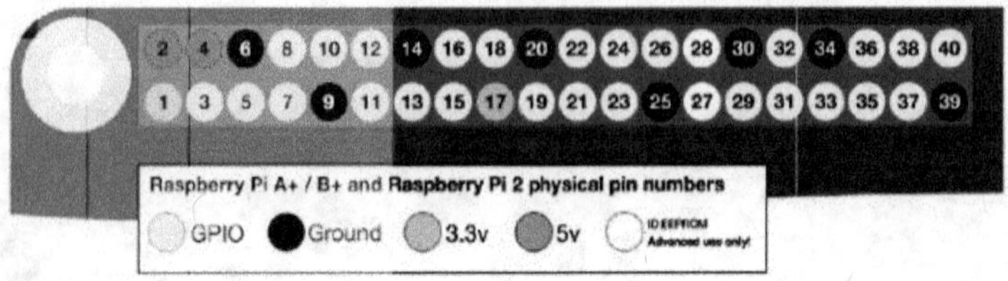

There are +5V (Pin 2 and 4) as well as +3.3V (Pin 1 and 17) control yield nails to the board for interfacing different modules and sensors. These power rails can't be utilized to drive the Stepper Motor, since we need more capacity to pivot it. So we need to convey the ability to Stepper Motor from another power source. My stepper engine has a voltage rating of 9V so I am utilizing a 9v battery as my subsequent power source. Search your stepper engine model number to realize voltage rating. Contingent upon the rating pick the auxiliary source fittingly.

As expressed before, we need a driver circuit to drive the Stepper Motor. We will likewise be structuring a Simple Transistor Driver Circuit here.

Components Required:

Here we are utilizing Raspberry Pi two Model B with Raspbian Jessie OS. All the fundamental Hardware and Software prerequisites are recently talked about, you can find it in the Raspberry Pi Introduction, other than that we need:

- Connecting pins

- 220? or 1K?resistor (3)
- Stepper Motor
- 2N2222 Transistor (4)
- Buttons (2)
- 1N4007 Diode (4)
- Bread Board
- Capacitor- 1000uF

Circuit Explanation:

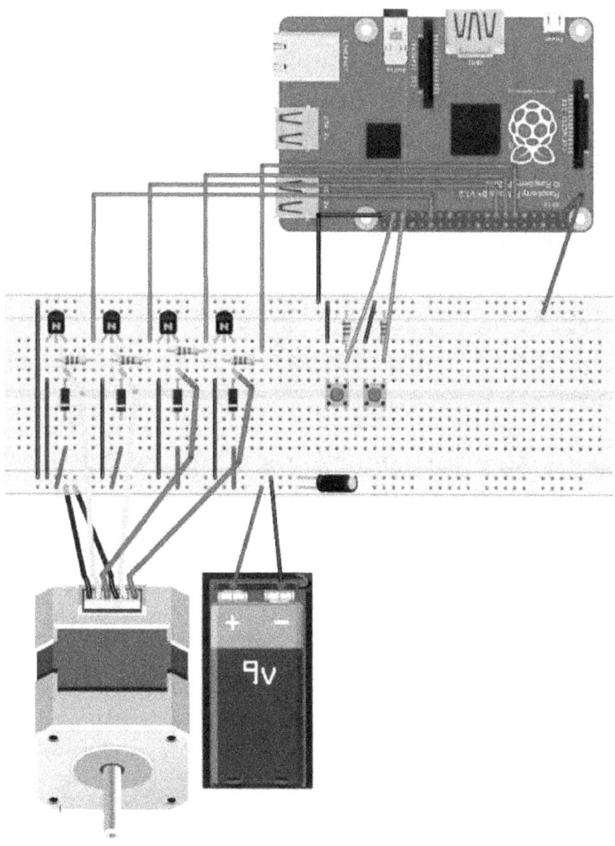

Stepper engine utilize 200 stages to finish 360 degree turn, implies its pivot 1.8 degree per step. As we are driving a Four Stage Stepper Motor, so we have to give four heartbeats to finish single rationale cycle. Each progression of this engine finishes 1.8 level of revolution, so as to finish a cycle we need 200 heartbeats. So 200/4 = 50 rationale cycles expected to finish a solitary turn. Check this to find out about Steppers Motors and its Driving Modes.

We will be driving every one of these four loops by a NPN transistor (2N2222), this NPN transistor takes the rationale beat from PI and drives the comparing curl. Four transistors are taking four rationales from PI to drive four phases of stepper engine.

The transistor driver circuit is a precarious arrangement; here we should focus that wrongly interfacing the transistor may stack the board intensely and harm it. Check this to appropriately comprehend the Stepper Motor Driver Circuit.

The engine is an enlistment thus while exchanging the engine, we experience inductive spiking. This spiking will warm up the transistor vigorously, so we will utilize Diode (1N4007) to give security to transistor against Inductive Spiking.

So as to diminish the voltage variances, we will associate a 1000uF capacitor over the power supply as appeared in the Circuit Diagram.

Working Explanation:

Once everything is associated according to the circuit chart, we can turn ON the PI to compose the program in PYHTON.

We will discuss scarcely any directions which we are gonna to use in PYHTON program,

We are gonna to import General Purpose Input Output record from library, beneath work empowers us to program GPIO pins of PI. We are additionally renaming "GPIO" to "IO", so in the program at whatever point we need to allude to GPIO pins we will utilize the word 'IO'.

```
import RPi.GPIO as IO
```

In some cases, when the GPIO pins, which we are attempting to utilize, may be doing some different capacities. All things considered, we will get admonitions while executing the program. Beneath direction advises the PI to disregard the alerts and continue with the program.

```
IO.setwarnings(False)
```

We can allude the General Purpose Input Output pins of PI, either by nail number to board otherwise by their capacity number. Like 'PIN 35' on the board is

'GPIO19'. So we advise here possibly we will speak to the pin here by '35' or '19'.

```
IO.setmode (IO.BCM)
```

We are setting four of GPIO sticks as yield for driving four curls of stepper engine.

```
IO.setup(5,IO.OUT)

IO.setup(17,IO.OUT)

IO.setup(27,IO.OUT)

IO.setup(22,IO.OUT)
```

We are setting GPIO26 and GPIO19 as info pins. We will distinguish button press by these pins.

```
IO.setup(19,IO.IN)

IO.setup(26,IO.IN)
```

In case the Condition in the supports is valid, the announcements inside the circle will be executed once. So in the event that the GPIO pin 26 goes low, at that point the announcements inside the IF circle will be executed once. On the off chance that the GPIO pin 26 doesn't goes low, at that point the announcements inside the IF circle won't be executed.

```
if(IO.input(26) = = False):
```

This order executes the circle multiple times, x being augmented from 0 to 99.

```
for x in range (100):
```

While 1: is utilized for boundlessness circle. With this direction the announcements inside this circle will be executed persistently.

We have every one of the directions expected to accomplish the Speed Control of Stepper Motor with this.

In the wake of composing the program and executing, everything there is left is working the control. We have two catches associated with PI. One for increases the postponement between the four heartbeats and other for decrements the deferral between the four heartbeats. The postpone itself talks about speed; if the deferral is higher the engine makes brakes between each stride thus revolution is moderate. In the event that the deferral is almost zero, at that point the engine turns at greatest speed.

Here it ought to be recall that, there ought to be some postponement between the beats. Subsequent to giving a heartbeat, stepper engine sets aside scarcely any milliseconds of effort to arrive at its last stage. In the event that there is no defer given between the beats, the stepper engine won't move by any means. Regularly 50ms deferral is fine between the beats. For increasingly exact data, investigate the information sheet.

So with two catches we can control the postponement, which in turns control the speed of the stepper engine.

Code

```
import RPi.GPIO as IO       # we are calling for header
file which helps us use GPIO's of PI
import time                 # we are calling for time to
provide delays in program
IO.setwarnings(False)       # do not show any warnings
x=1                         # integer for storing the delay
multiple
IO.setmode (IO.BCM)
IO.setup(5,IO.OUT)          # initialize GPIO5 as an out-
put.
IO.setup(17,IO.OUT)
IO.setup(27,IO.OUT)
IO.setup(22,IO.OUT)
```

```python
IO.setup(19,IO.IN)              # initialize GPIO19 as an input.
IO.setup(26,IO.IN)
while 1:                  # execute loop forever
  IO.output(5,1)              # Step1 go high
  IO.output(22,0)
  for y in range(x):         # sleep for x*100msec
    time.sleep(0.01)
  IO.output(17,1)            # step2 go high
  IO.output(5,0)
  for y in range(x):
    time.sleep(0.01)         # sleep for x*100msec
  IO.output(27,1)            #step 3 go high
  IO.output(17,0)
  for y in range(x):
    time.sleep(0.01)         # sleep for x*100msec
  IO.output(22,1)            #step 4 go high
  IO.output(27,0)
  for y in range(x):
    time.sleep(0.01)                # sleep for x*100msec
    if(IO.input(26) == False):      #if button1 is pressed
     if(x<100):
      x=x+1                         #increment x by one if x<100
      time.sleep(0.5)               #sleep for 500ms

     if(IO.input(19) == False):     #if button2 is pressed
      if(x>1):
       x=x-1                        #decrement x by one if x>1
       time.sleep(0.5)              #sleep for 500ms
```

8. DC MOTOR CONTROL WITH RASPBERRY PI

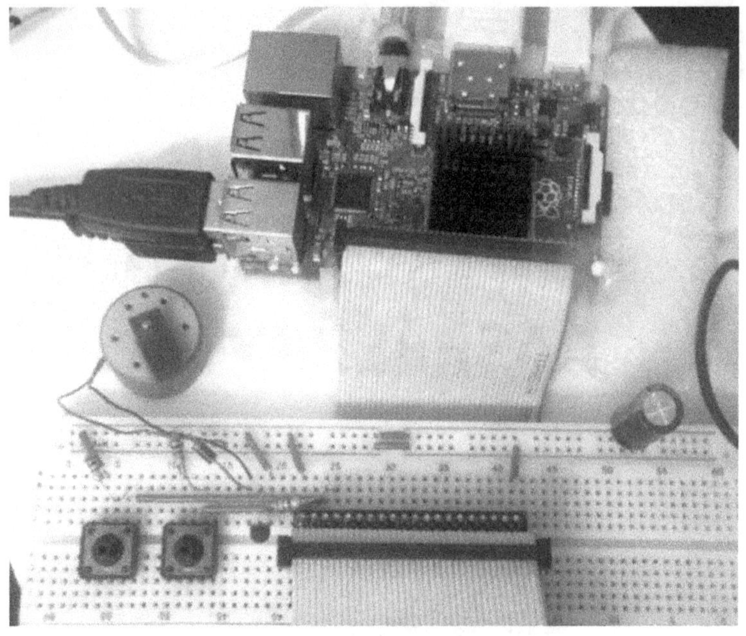

Raspberry Pi is an ARM design processor based board intended for electronic specialists and specialists. The PI is one of most confided in venture improvement stages out there now. With higher processor speed and 1 GB RAM, the PI can be used for some, prominent ventures like Image preparing and Internet of Things.

For doing any of prominent tasks, one have to comprehend the essential elements of PI. We will cover all the fundamental functionalities of Raspberry Pi in these instructional exercises. In every instructional exercise we will talk about one of elements of PI. Before the finish of instructional exercise arrangement you will have the option to do prominent undertakings without anyone else. Check these for Getting Initiated with Raspberry Pi as well as Raspberry Pi Configuration.

We have talked about LED Blinky, Button Interfacing and PWM age in past instructional exercises. In this instructional exercise we will Control the Speed of a DC engine utilizing Raspberry Pi and PWM strategy. (Pulse Width Modulation) is a strategy utilized for getting variable voltage out of consistent power source. We have talked about PWM in the past instructional exercise.

There are 40 GPIO yield sticks in Raspberry Pi 2. Yet, out of 40, just 26 GPIO pins (GPIO2 to GPIO27) can be customized. A portion of these pins play out some unique capacities. With unique GPIO set aside, we have 17 GPIO remaining. To find out about GPIO pins, experience: LED Blinking with Raspberry Pi

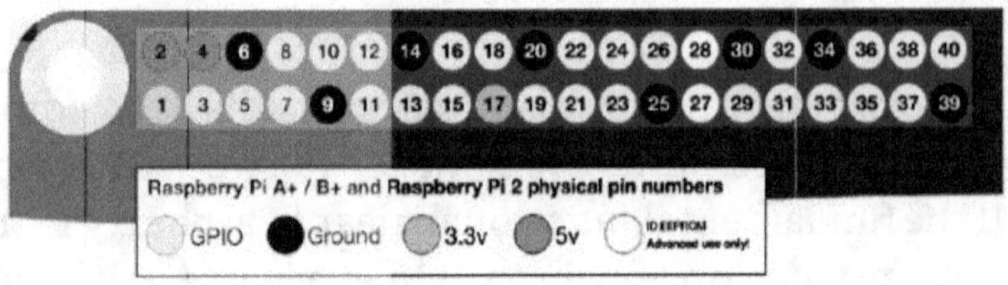

Every one of these 17 GPIO pin can convey a limit of 15mA. What's more, the total of flows from all GPIO Pins can't surpass 50mA. So we can attract a limit of 3mA normal from every one of these GPIO pins. So one ought not mess with these things except if you comprehend what you are doing.

There are +5V (Pin 2 and 4) and +3.3V (Pin 1 and 17) control yield nails to the board for interfacing different modules and sensors. This power rail is associated in parallel to processor control. So drawing High current from this power rail influences the Processor. There is a breaker on the PI board which will trip once you apply high burden. You can draw 100mA securely from the +3.3V rail. We are discussing this here in light of the fact that; we are associating the DC engine to +3.3V. In light of as far as possible, we can just interface low power engine here, in the event that you need to drive high power engine, consider controlling it from a different power source.

Components Required:

Here we are utilizing Raspberry Pi two Model B with Raspbian Jessie OS. All the essential Hardware and

Software necessities are recently talked about, you can find it in the Raspberry Pi Introduction, other than that we need:

- Connecting pins
- 220? or 1K? resistor (3)
- Small DC Motor
- Buttons (two)
- 1N4007 Diode
- 2N2222 Transistor
- Bread Board
- Capacitor- 1000uF

Circuit Explanation:

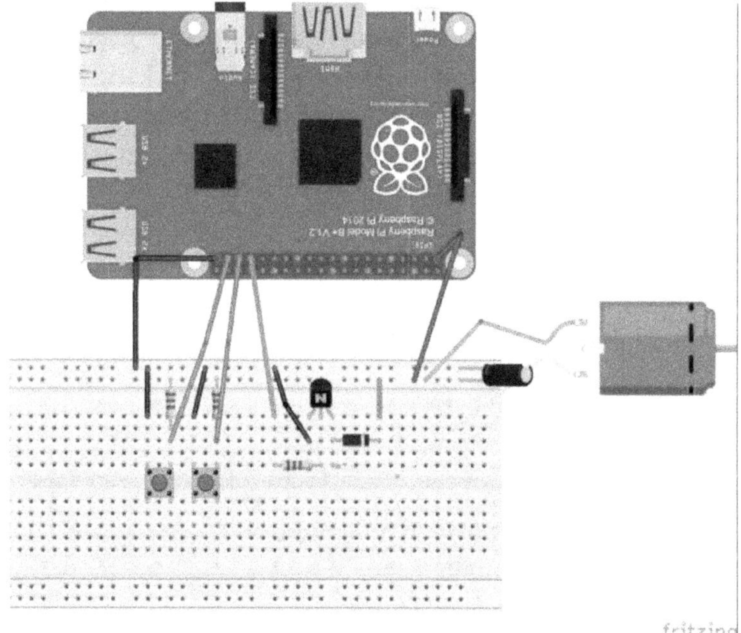

As said before, we can't draw more than 15mA from any General Purpose Input Output pins as well as Direct Current engine draws more than 15mA, so the Pulse Width Modulation produced by Raspberry Pi can't be sustained to the DC engine legitimately. So in case we interface the engine legitimately to PI for speed control, the board may get harmed for all time.

So we are going to utilize a NPN transistor (2N2222) as an exchanging gadget. This transistor here drives the powerful DC engine by taking PWM signal from PI. Here one should focus that wrongly interfacing the transistor may stack the board vigorously.

The engine is an enlistment thus while exchanging the engine, we experience inductive spiking. This spiking will warm up the transistor intensely, so we will utilize Diode (1N4007) to give insurance to transistor against Inductive Spiking.

So as to diminish the voltage vacillations, we will associate a 1000uF capacitor over the power supply as appeared in the Circuit Diagram.

Working Explanation:

Once everything is associated according to the circuit chart, we can turn ON the PI to compose the program in PYHTON.
We will discuss scarcely any directions which we are gonna to use in PYHTON program.

We are gonna to import General Purpose Input Output document from library, underneath work empowers us to program General Purpose Input Output pins of PI. We are additionally renaming "GPIO" to "IO", so in the program at whatever point we need to allude to GPIO pins we will utilize the word 'IO'.

```
import RPi.GPIO as IO
```

Now and again, when the GPIO pins, which we are attempting to utilize, may be doing some different capacities. All things considered, we will get alerts while executing the program. Underneath order advises the PI to disregard the alerts and continue with the program.

```
IO.setwarnings(False)
```

We can allude the General Purpose Input Output pins of PI, either by nail number to board otherwise by their capacity number. Like 'PIN 35' on the board is 'GPIO19'. So we advise here it is possible that we will speak to the pin here by '35' or '19'.

```
IO.setmode (IO.BCM)
```

We are setting GPIO19 (or PIN35) as yield pin. We will get PWM yield from this pin.

```
IO.setup(19,IO.IN)
```

In the wake of setting the pin as yield we have to arrangement the pin as PWM yield pin,

```
p = IO.PWM(output channel , frequency of PWM signal)
```

The above order is for setting up the channel and furthermore for setting up the recurrence of the PWM signal. 'p' here is a variable it very well may be anything. We are utilizing GPIO19 as the PWM yield channel. 'recurrence of PWM signal' has been picked 100, as we would prefer not to see LED flickering.

Beneath order is utilized to begin PWM signal age, 'DUTYCYCLE' is for setting the Turn On proportion, 0 methods LED will be ON for 0% of time, 30 methods LED will be ON for 30% of the time and 100 methods totally ON.

```
p.start(DUTYCYCLE)
```

In case the Condition in the supports is valid, the announcements inside the circle will be executed once. So on the off chance that the GPIO pin 26 goes low, at that point the announcements inside the IF circle will be executed once. On the off chance that the GPIO pin 26 doesn't goes low, at that point the announcements inside the IF circle won't be executed.

```
if(IO.input(26) == False):
```

While 1: is utilized for boundlessness circle. With this direction the announcements inside this circle will be executed consistently.

We have every one of the directions expected to accomplish the speed control with this.

A s a result of composing the program and executing, everything there is left is working the control. We have two catches associated with PI; one for increasing the Duty Cycle of PWM signal and other for decrementing the Duty Cycle of PWM signal. By squeezing one catch the, speed of DC engine increments and by squeezing the other catch, the speed of DC engine diminishes. With this we have accomplished the DC Motor Speed Control by Raspberry Pi.

Additionally check:

- Direct Current Motor Speed Control
- DC Motor Control utilizing Arduino

Code

```
import RPi.GPIO as IO      # calling header file which
helps us use GPIO's of PI

import time                # calling time to provide delays
in program

IO.setwarnings(False)      #do not show any warnings

x=0                        #integer for storing the duty cycle
value

IO.setmode (IO.BCM)        #we are programming the
GPIO by BCM pin numbers. (PIN35 as'GPIO19')

IO.setup(13,IO.OUT)        # initialize GPIO13 as an out-
put.
IO.setup(19,IO.IN)         # initialize GPIO19 as an input.
IO.setup(26,IO.IN)         # initialize GPIO26 as an input.

p = IO.PWM(13,100)         #GPIO13 as PWM output, with
100Hz frequency
p.start(0)                 #generate PWM signal with 0%
duty cycle

while 1:                   #execute loop forever

  p.ChangeDutyCycle(x)         #change duty cycle for
changing the brightness of LED.
  if(IO.input(26) == False):    #if button1 is pressed
    if(x<50):
      x=x+1                     #increment x by one if x<50
      time.sleep(0.2)          #sleep for 200ms
```

```
if(IO.input(19) == False):      #if button2 is pressed
   if(x>0):
     x=x-1                      #decrement x by one if x>0
     time.sleep(0.2)           #sleep for 200ms
```

❖ ❖ ❖

9. RASPBERRY PI PWM TUTORIAL

Raspberry Pi is an ARM engineering processor based board intended for electronic designers and specialists. The PI is one of most confided in venture improvement stages out there now. With higher processor speed as well as one Giga Byte Random Access Memory, the PI can be utilized for some, prominent ventures like Image handling and Internet of Things.

For doing any of prominent activities, one have to comprehend the essential elements of PI. We will cover all the fundamental functionalities of Raspberry Pi in these instructional exercises. In every instructional exercise we will talk about one of elements of PI. Before the finish of instructional exercise arrangement you will have the choice to do prominent tasks without anyone else's input. Check these for Getting Initiated with Raspberry Pi as well as Raspberry Pi Configuration.

We have talked about LED blinky and Button interface with Raspberry Pi in past instructional exercises. In this Raspberry Pi PWM instructional exercise we will discuss getting PWM yield with Raspberry Pi. PWM means 'Heartbeat Width Modulation'. PWM is a technique utilized for getting variable voltage out of consistent power supply. We will produce PWM signal from Raspberry PI and exhibit the PWM by differing the Brightness of a LED, associated with Pi.

Pulse Width Modulation:

We have recently discussed PWM commonly in: Pulse width Modulation with ATmega32 , PWM with Arduino Uno, PWM with 555 clock IC and PWM with Arduino Due.

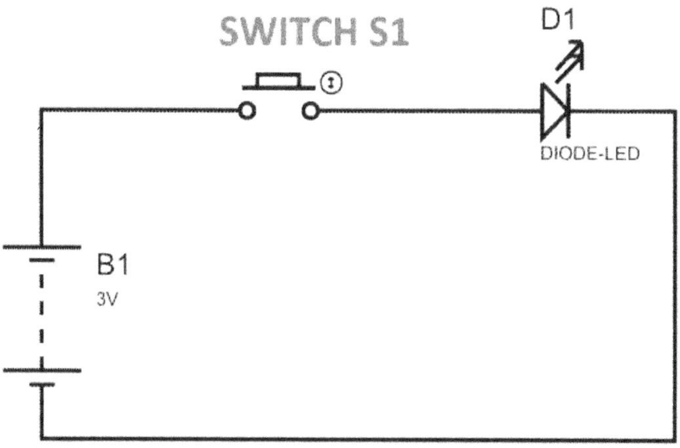

In above figure, if the switch is shut persistently over some undefined time frame, the LED will be 'ON' during this time consistently. In the event that the switch is shut for half second and opened for next half second, at that point LED will be ON just in the main half second. Presently the extent for which the LED is ON over the absolute time is known as the Duty Cycle, and can be determined as pursues:

Obligation Cycle =Turn ON schedule/(Turn ON time + Turn OFF time)

Obligation Cycle = (0.5/ (0.5+0.5)) = half

So the normal yield voltage will be half of the battery voltage.

This is the situation for 1 sec as well as we can view the Light Emitting Diode being OFF for half sec as well as Light Emitting Diode being ON the other half sec.

On the off chance that Frequency of ON and OFF occasions expanded from '1 every second' to '50 every second'. The human eye can't catch this recurrence. For an ordinary eye the LED will be seen, as shining with half of the brilliance. So with further decrease of ON time the LED shows up a lot lighter.

We will program the PI for getting a PWM and associate a LED to show its working.

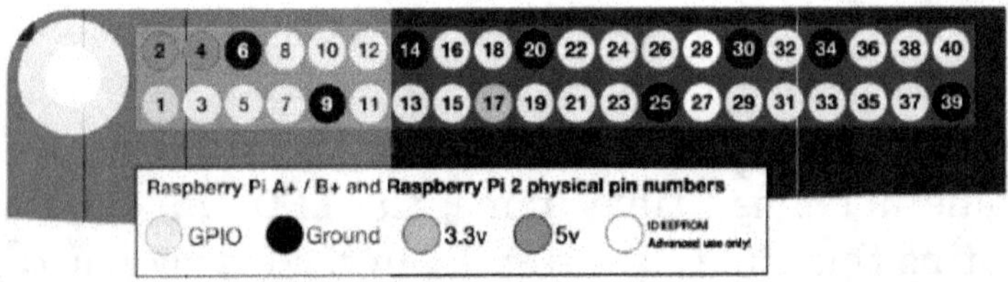

There are 40 GPIO yield sticks in Raspberry Pi. Be that as it may, out of 40, just 26 GPIO pins (GPIO2 to GPIO27) can be customized. TO find out about GPIO pins, experience: LED Blinking with Raspberry Pi

Components Required:

Here we are utilizing Raspberry Pi two Model B with Raspbian Jessie OS. All the essential Hardware and Software prerequisites are recently talked about, you can find it in the Raspberry Pi Introduction, other than that we need:

- Connecting pins

- 220? or 1K?resistor
- LED
- Bread Board

Circuit Explanation:

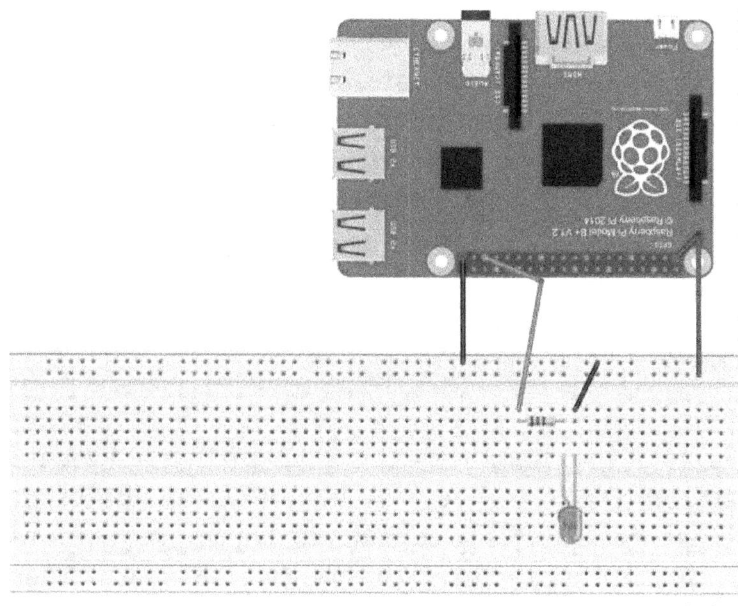

As appeared in the circuit chart we will associate a LED between PIN35 (GPIO19) and PIN39 (ground). As said before, we can't draw more than 15mA from any of these pins, so to confine the present we are associating a 220? or 1K? resistor in arrangement with the LED.

Working Explanation:

Once everything is associated, we can turn ON the Raspberry Pi to compose the program in PYHTON and execute it.

We will discuss scarcely any directions which we are gonna to use in PYHTON program.

We are gonna to import General Purpose Input Output document from library, beneath work empowers us to program General Purpose Input Output pins of PI. We are additionally renaming "GPIO" to "IO", so in the program at whatever point we need to allude to GPIO pins we will utilize the word 'IO'.

```
import RPi.GPIO as IO
```

Some of the time, when the GPIO pins, which we are attempting to utilize, may be doing some different capacities. All things considered, we will get admonitions while executing the program. Beneath order advises the PI to disregard the alerts and continue with the program.

```
IO.setwarnings(False)
```

We can allude the General Purpose Input Output pins of PI, either by nail number to board otherwise by their capacity number. In pin chart, you can see 'PIN

35' on the board is 'GPIO19'. So we advise here it is possible that we will speak to the pin here by '35' or '19'.

```
IO.setmode (IO.BCM)
```

We are setting GPIO19 (or PIN35) as yield pin. We will get PWM yield from this pin.

```
IO.setup(19,IO.IN)
```

Subsequent to setting the pin as yield we have to arrangement the pin as PWM yield pin,

```
p = IO.PWM(output channel , frequency of PWM signal)
```

The above direction is for setting up the channel and furthermore for setting up the recurrence of the PWM signal. 'p' here is a variable it very well may be anything. We are utilizing GPIO19 as the PWM yield channel. 'recurrence of PWM signal' has been picked 100, as we would prefer not to see LED flickering.

Beneath order is utilized to begin PWM signal age, 'DUTYCYCLE' is for setting the Turn On proportion, 0 methods LED will be ON for 0% of time, 30 methods

LED will be ON for 30% of the time and 100 methods totally ON.

```
p.start(DUTYCYCLE)
```

This order executes the circle multiple times, x being augmented from 0 to 49.

```
for x in range (50):
```

While 1: is utilized for boundlessness circle. With this direction the announcements inside this circle will be executed consistently.

With the program being executed, the obligation cycle of PWM signal increments. And afterward diminishes as a result of arriving at 100%. With a LED connected to this PIN, brilliance of LED builds first and afterward diminishes.

Code

import RPi.GPIO as IO   #calling header file which helps us use GPIO's of PI

import time   #calling time to provide delays in program

IO.setwarnings(False)   #do not show any warnings

IO.setmode (IO.BCM)   #we are programming the

GPIO by BCM pin numbers. (PIN35 as 'GPIO19')

```
IO.setup(19,IO.OUT)          # initialize GPIO19 as an
output.

p = IO.PWM(19,100)           #GPIO19 as PWM output,
with 100Hz frequency
p.start(0)                   #generate PWM signal with 0%
duty cycle

while 1:                     #execute loop forever

    for x in range (50):            #execute loop for 50
times, x being incremented from 0 to 49.
    p.ChangeDutyCycle(x)        #change duty cycle for
varying the brightness of LED.
    time.sleep(0.1)             #sleep for 100m second


    for x in range (50):            #execute loop for 50
times, x being incremented from 0 to 49.
    p.ChangeDutyCycle(50-x)     #change duty cycle for
changing the brightness of LED.
    time.sleep(0.1)             #sleep for 100m second
```

10. INTERFACE A CATCH TO RASPBERRY PI

Raspberry Pi is an ARM design processor based board intended for electronic architects and specialists. The PI is one of most confided in venture improvement stages out there now. With higher processor speed and 1 GB RAM, the PI can be utilized for some, prominent undertakings like Image handling and Internet of Things.

For doing any of prominent tasks, one have to comprehend the essential elements of PI. That is the reason we are here, we will cover all the fundamental functionalities of Raspberry Pi in these instructional exercises. In every instructional exercise arrangement we will talk about one of elements of PI. Before the finish of instructional exercise arrangement you will have the choice to do prominent activities independent from anyone else. Check these for Getting Initiated with Raspberry Pi as well as Raspberry Pi Configuration.

Setting up correspondence among PI and client is significant for planning ventures on PI. For the correspondence, PI must take Inputs from the client. In this second instructional exercise of PI arrangement, we will Interface a catch to Raspberry Pi, to take INPUTS from the client.

Here we will interface a catch to one GPIO Pin and a LED to another GPIO pin of Raspberry Pi. We will compose a program in PYTHON, to squint the LED constantly, on squeezing the catch by the client. Driven will be squinting by killing the GPIO On and.

Prior to going for the writing computer programs, how about we talk somewhat about the LINUX and PYHTON.

LINUX:

LINUX is an Operating System like Windows. It plays out all the essential capacities which Windows OS can do. The principle contrast between them is, Linux is open source programming where Windows isn't. What it fundamentally implies is, Linux is free while Windows isn't. Linux OS can be downloaded and worked for nothing, yet for downloading certifiable Windows OS, you need to pay the cash.

Also, another significant distinction between them is

Linux OS can be 'changed' by tweaking into the code, however Windows OS can't be altered, doing so will prompt lawful confusions. So anybody can take the Linux OS, and can alter it to his necessity so as to make his own OS. In any case, we can't do this in Windows, the Windows OS is furnished with limitations to prevent you from altering OS.

Here we are discussing Linux in light of the fact that, JESSIE LITE (Raspberry Pi OS) is LINUX based OS, which we have introduced in Raspberry Pi Introduction part. The PI OS is created on the grounds of LINUX, so we need to realize somewhat about LINUX working directions. We will talk about these Linux directions in the accompanying instructional exercises.

PYTHON:

In contrast to LINUX, PYTHON is a programming language like C, C++, and JAVA and so on. These dialects are utilized to create applications. Recall programming dialects run on Operating System. You can't run a programming language without an OS. So OS is autonomous while programming dialects are reliant. You can run PYTHON, C, C++, and JAVA on both Linux and Windows.

Applications created by these programming dialects can be games, programs, applications and so on. We will utilize programming language PYTHON on our PI, to configuration ventures and to control the

GPIO's.

We will talk about somewhat about PI GPIO before going any further,

GPIO Pins:

As appeared in above figure, there are 40output pins for the PI. Be that as it may, when you take a gander at the subsequent figure, you can see not every one of the 40 pin out can be modified to our utilization.

These are just 26 GPIO pins which can be customized. These pins go from GPIO2 to GPIO27.

These 26 GPIO pins can be modified according to require. A portion of these pins likewise play out some uncommon capacities, we will talk about that later. With uncommon GPIO set aside, we have 17 GPIO staying (Light green Cirl).

Every one of these 17 GPIO pins can convey a limit of 15mA current. What's more, the total of flows from all GPIO can't surpass 50mA. So we can attract a limit of 3mA normal from every one of these GPIO pins. So one ought not mess with these things except if you comprehend what you are doing.

Components Required:

Here we are utilizing Raspberry Pi 2 Model B with Raspbian Jessie OS. All the essential Hardware and Software prerequisites are recently talked about, you can find it in the Raspberry Pi Introduction, other than that we need:

- Connecting pins
- 220? or 1K?resistor
- LED
- Button
- Bread Board

Circuit Explanation:

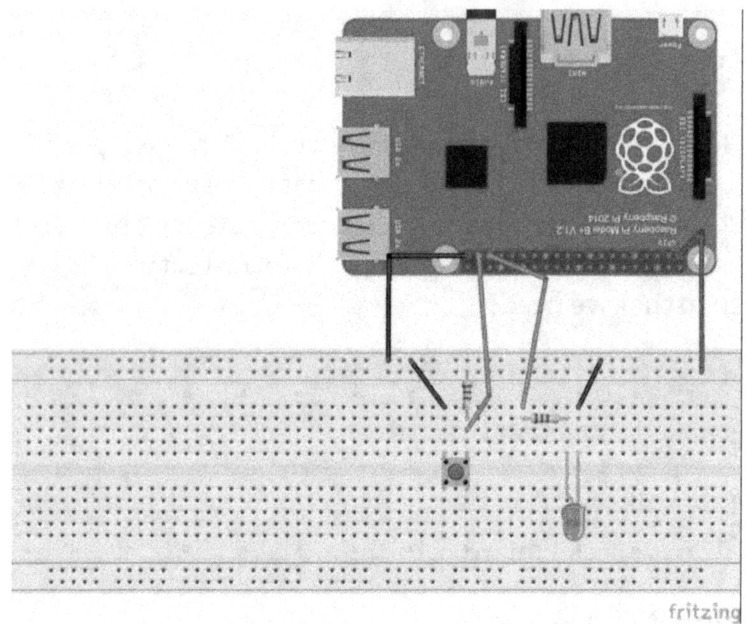

As appeared in the circuit chart we will interface a LED to PIN35 (GPIO19) and a catch to PIN37 (GPIO26). As said before, we can't draw more than 15mA from any of these pins, so to constrain the present we are interfacing a 220? or 1K? resistor in arrangement with the LED.

Working Explanation:

Once everything is associated, we can turn ON the Raspberry Pi to compose the program in PYHTON and execute it. (To realize how to utilize PYTHON go to PI BLINKY).

We will discuss not many directions which we are going to use in PYHTON program.

We are going to import GPIO record from library, underneath work empowers us to program GPIO pins of PI. We are likewise renaming "GPIO" to "IO", so in the program at whatever point we need to allude to GPIO pins we will utilize the word 'IO'.

```
import RPi.GPIO as IO
```

Now and again, when the GPIO pins, which we are attempting to utilize, may be doing some different capacities. All things considered, we will get admonitions while executing the program. Beneath direction advises the PI to disregard the admonitions and continue with the program.

```
IO.setwarnings(False)
```

We can allude the GPIO pins of PI, either by nail number to board or by their capacity number. In pin chart, you can see 'PIN 37' on the board is 'GPIO26'. So we advise here it is possible that we will speak to the pin here by '37' or '26'.

```
IO.setmode (IO.BCM)
```

We are setting GPIO26 (or PIN37) as info pin. We will identify button press by this pin.

```
IO.setup(26,IO.IN)
```

While 1: is utilized for boundlessness circle. With this order the announcements inside this circle will be executed constantly.

When the program is executed, the LED associated with GPIO19 (PIN35) squints at whatever point the catch is squeezed. Upon discharge the LED, it will go to OFF state once more.

Code

```
import RPi.GPIO as IO        #we are calling header file which helps us to use GPIO's of PI

import time                  # we are calling for time to provide delays in program

IO.setwarnings(False)        #do not show any warnings

IO.setmode (IO.BCM)          #we are programming the GPIO by BCM pin numbers. (PIN39 as 'GPIO19')

IO.setup(19,IO.OUT)          # initialize GPIO19 as an output.

IO.setup(26,IO.IN)           #initialize GPIO26 as input

while 1:                     #execute loop forever
```

```
    if(IO.input(26) == False):    #if GPIO26 goes low exe-
cute the below statements
        IO.output(19,True)        # turn the LED on (making
the voltage level HIGH)
        time.sleep(0.11)          #sleep for 100m second
        IO.output(19,False)       # turn the LED off (making
GPIO19 low)
        time.sleep(1)             #sleep for 100m second
```

11. DRIVEN BLINKING WITH RASPBERRY PI AS WELL AS PYTHON PROGRAM

Raspberry Pi is an ARM design processor based board intended for electronic specialists and specialists. The PI is one of most confided in venture improvement stages out there now. With higher processor speed and 1 GB RAM, the PI can be used for some, prominent ventures like Image handling and Internet of Things.

For doing any of prominent activities, one have to comprehend the fundamental elements of PI. That is the reason we are here, we will show all the essential functionalities of Raspberry Pi in these instructional exercises. In every instructional exercise arrangement we will talk about one of elements of PI. Before the finish of instructional exercise arrangement you will have the option to do prominent activities without anyone else. Check these for Getting Initiated with Raspberry Pi as well as Raspberry Pi Configuration.

In this instructional exercise of PI arrangement, we will comprehend the idea of composing and executing programs on PYTHON. We will begin with Blink Light Emitting Diode utilizing Raspberry Pi. Blinky is finished by interfacing a Light Emitting Diode to one of General Purpose Input Output pins of PI as well as turning it ON as well as OFF.

We will talk about somewhat about PI General Purpose Input Output Pins before going any further,

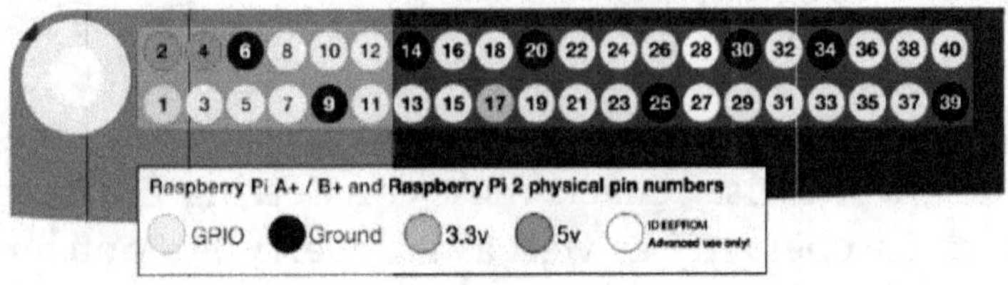

As appeared in above figure, there are 40output pins for the PI. In any case, when you take a gander at the subsequent figure, you can view not each of the 40 pin out can be customized to our utilization. These are just 26 GPIO pins which can be customized. These pins go from GPIO2 to GPIO27.

These 26 GPIO pins can be customized according to require. A portion of these pins likewise play out some exceptional capacities, we will talk about that later. With uncommon GPIO set aside, we have 17 GPIO staying (Light green Cirl).

Every one of these 17 GPIO pins can convey a limit of 15mA current. What's more, the total of flows from all GPIO can't surpass 50mA. So we can attract a limit of 3mA normal from every one of these GPIO pins. So one ought not alter these things except if you comprehend what you are doing.

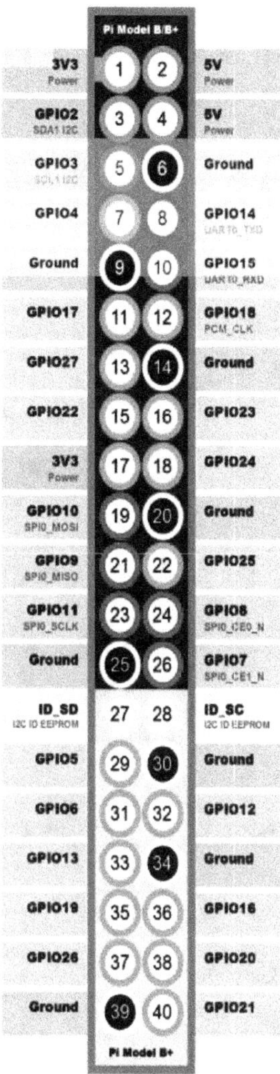

Components Required:

Here we are utilizing Raspberry Pi 2 Model B with Raspbian Jessie OS. All the fundamental Hardware and Software necessities are recently talked about, you can find it in the Raspberry Pi Introduction, other than that we need:

- Connecting pins
- 220? or 1K?resistor
- LED
- Bread Board

Circuit Explanation:

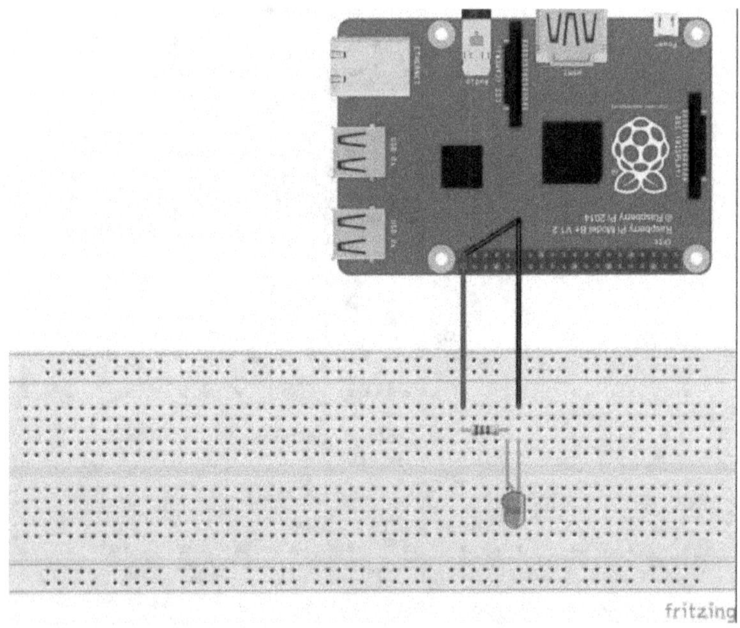

As appeared in the circuit graph we will associate a LED between PIN40 (GPIO21) and PIN39 (GROUND). As said before, we can't draw more than 15mA from any of these pins, so to restrict the present we are associating a 220? or 1K? resistor in arrangement with the LED.

Working Explanation:

Since we have everything prepared, turn ON your PI and go to the work area.

1. On the work area, go the Start Menu as well as decide for the PYTHON three, as appeared in figure underneath.

2. From that point onward, PYHON will run and you will consider a to be as appeared in underneath figure.

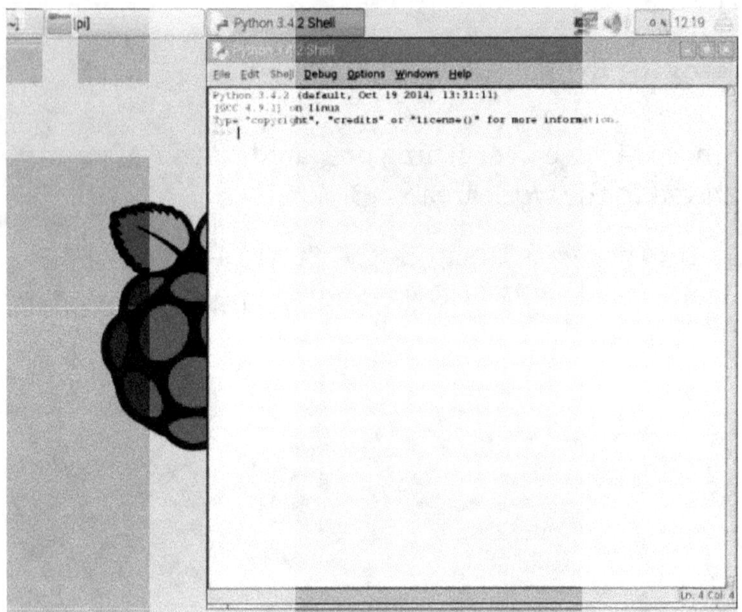

3. From that point forward, click on New File in File Menu, You will see another Window open,

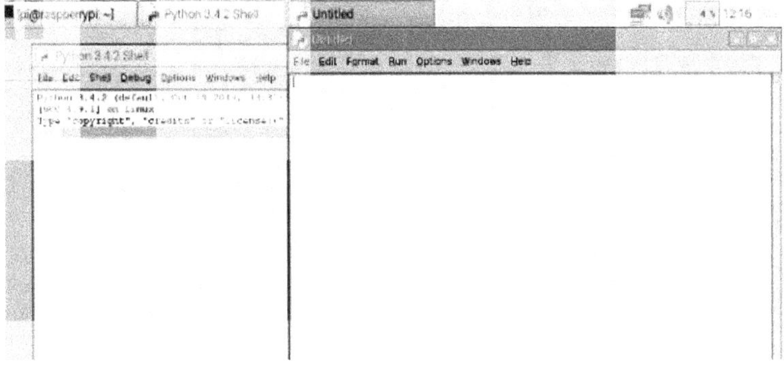

4. Spare this record as blinky on the work area,

5. After that compose the program for blinky as given beneath and execute the program by tapping on "RUN" on 'Troubleshoot' choice.

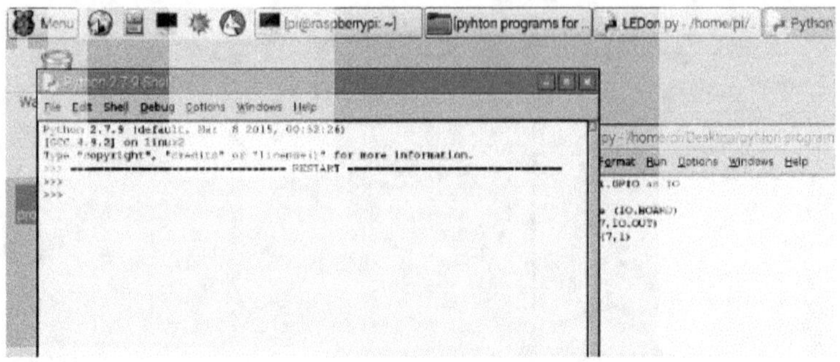

In case the program has no blunders in it, you will see a ">>>", which implies the program is executed effectively. At this point you should see the LED flickering multiple times. On the off chance that there were any mistakes in the program, the execution advises to address it. When the blunder is rectified execute the program once more.

We will see the PYTHON program Code for LED Blinking, in detail, beneath.

Code

```
import RPi.GPIO as IO        # calling header file for GPIO's of PI
import time                  # calling for time to provide delays in program

IO.setmode (IO.BOARD)        # programming the GPIO by BOARD pin numbers, GPIO21 is called as PIN40
IO.setup(40,IO.OUT)          # initialize digital pin40 as
```

```
an output.
IO.output(40,1)          # turn the LED on (making the
voltage level HIGH)
time.sleep(1)            # sleep for a second
IO.cleanup()             # turn the LED off (making all the
output pins LOW)
time.sleep(1)            #sleep for a second

#loop is executed second time
IO.setmode (IO.BOARD)
IO.setup(40,IO.OUT)
IO.output(40,1)
time.sleep(1)
IO.cleanup()
time.sleep(1)

#loop is executed third time
IO.setmode (IO.BOARD)
IO.setup(40,IO.OUT)
IO.output(40,1)
time.sleep(1)
IO.cleanup()
time.sleep(1)
```

12. BEGINNING WITH RASPBERRY PI - CONFIGURATION

In past session, we have found out about Raspberry Pi board, its ports, its equipment and programming necessities and figured out how to introduce OS on Secure Digital card for PI.

When the OS (Raspbian Jessie) introduced Secure Digital card is embedded into the Raspberry Pi with the screen, console and mouse associated, we are prepared to boot the Jessie first time. For this specific OS you needn't bother with Ethernet association.

When the power is begun ON, you will see the power RED LED sparkling. The BLUE LED will begin flickering at this stage, this implies the OS (Operating System) is stacking and the PI is checking every one of the drivers.

At this point you will consider information to be the screen as demonstrated as follows,

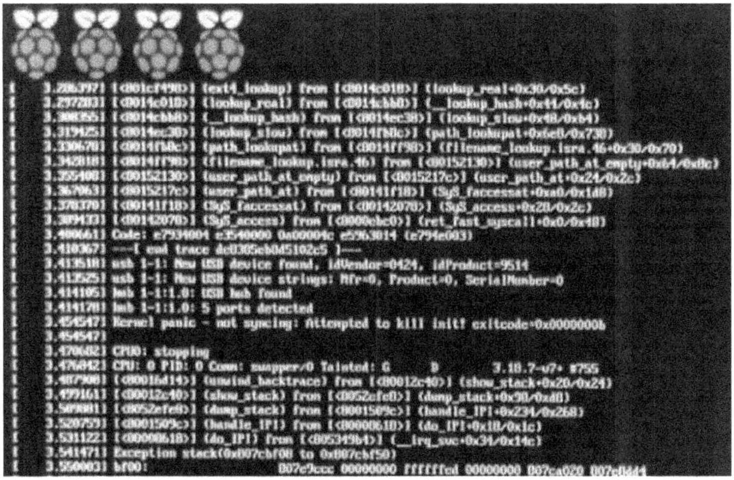

As told its equitable PI is stacking every one of the drives. You need to hold up until every one of the drivers are checked, if there should be an occurrence of blunder, turn now and again to restart PI. In the event that there is still inconvenience give introducing the OS a shot to the Secure Digital card again by following the means portrayed in first session.

In the case of everything goes effectively, you will be requested approval. This approval is predefined, with Username "pi" and secret phrase "raspberry",

USER: pi

```
< Press enter>

PASSWORD: raspberry

< Press enter>
```

When you enter these subtleties, you will be entered in CLI mode (Command Line) of Raspberry Pi. For going into the DESKTOP of PI you have to type,

```
startx

< Press enter>
```

BIOS settings:

Presently you have gone into the screen of Raspberry Pi and you are all set. Prior to going for the programming,

1. You have to arrange the BIOS settings of PI.

2. You have to arrange the console, you have picked.

In the event that you don't do these two things first you get parcel of blunders, while programming and working the PI.

For arranging the BIOS of PI first open the 'LX TERMINAL" of PI and enter this sudo raspi-config

< Press enter>

You will be gone into BIOS after this; you can watch beneath to perceive how it's finished.

The BIOS choices are as,

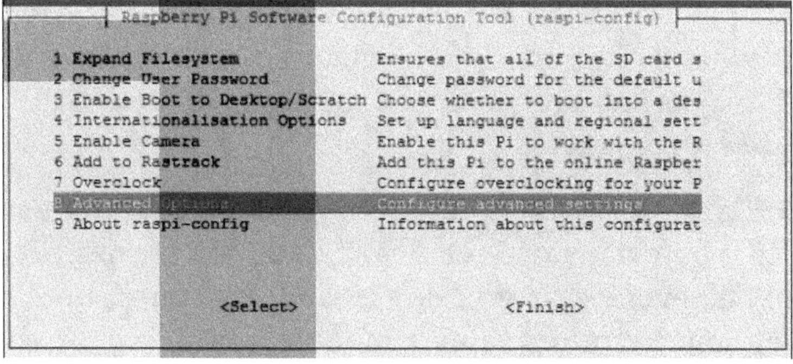

We will examine every one of these choices quickly underneath,

1. Grow File System: After first start, some memory of the Secure Digital will be lost and isn't considered by PI. You have to choose this alternative to get the records and request and to show the rest of the memory of SD card. When you pick this alternative, the PI will REBOOT to get everything all together. In case you don't grow the document framework, you won't have

the option to utilize remaining memory of SD card.

2. Change Password: This alternative changes the login secret key, its "pi" as a matter of course. Simply leave it, on the off chance that you are not doing any significant work.

3. Boot To Desktop: On the primary beginning you are entered in CLI mode, as talked about prior. This choice handicaps that, so you can enter DESKTOP of Pi with each start.

4. Internationalization Options: This alternative is for picking language. Its ENLGLISH naturally, leave it you would prefer not to change the language and date. The DATE might not be right, we will design theories settings later.

5. Empower Camera: If you have a camera module close by, arrange this choice. It will turn on the CAM. In the event that you don't have a camera, simply leave it. Recollect camera module draws control, so once you empower it the module will draw control persistently.

6. Add To Rastack: This alternative is for associating your PI on the web. Simply leave it.

7. Over Clock: This alternative over timekeepers PI, along these lines speeding up and furthermore its capacity utilization. Over timing may harm the board, if productive cooling framework isn't given. For essential programming, you need not over clock the PI, simply leave it 900MHz.

8. Propelled Options: These alternatives for BOARD gadgets (like AUDIO, I2C and so forth) design:

We have not many alternatives under this, however the significant until further notice is, 'Sound'. The PI can yield AUDIO either from HEADPHONE jack (on the PI board) or from HDMI port. To discover the ports, check Getting Initiated with Raspberry Pi. Pick the suitable one dependent on you utilization. In case you won't arrange this, you won't get AUDIO. The rest of the choices are not significant for the present.

The propelled choices are recorded as appeared underneath,

That is it you have arranged the PI BIOS settings.

Keyboard Configuring:

We utilize distinctive sort of console all around the globe, the large major of the keys coordinate for all consoles. In any case, hardly any keys confuse. This will raise truly ruckus while programming, as un-common keys have a critical influence while doing programming in PYTHON and LINUX. So we have to arrange the Raspberry Pi to the console we are utilizing. I am from INDIA and nearly everybody one here uses US (United States) console models.

So I am designing this on the 'Console Layout' choice,

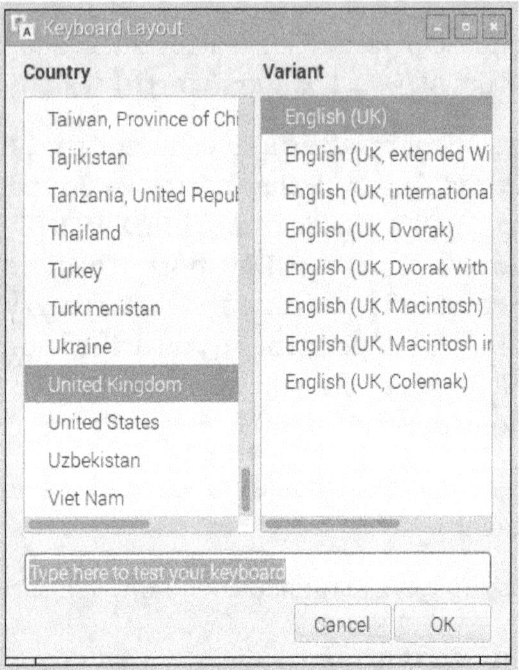

Beneath I will give you how I designed my console in detail,

Errors:

Now and again you will have white outskirts at the corners of the screen, you can choose them by RIGHT MOUSE BUTTON and erase then by LEFT MOUSE BUTTON.

So we have learnt rudiments of Raspberry pi in these two instructional exercises, presently in next instructional exercise we will flicker a LED with Raspberry Pi

13. BEGINNING WITH RASPBERRY PI - INTRODUCTION

Raspberry Pi is an ARM cortex based board intended for Electronic Engineers and Hobbyists. It's a solitary board PC chipping away at low power. With the preparing rate and memory, Raspberry Pi can be used for performing various capacities one after another, similar to a typical PC, and subsequently it is called Mini Computer in your palm.

Since it has an ARMv7 processor, it can run the full scope of ARM GNU/Linux appropriations just as Microsoft Windows 10, we will examine about that later. ARM engineering is compelling in current hardware. We are utilizing the ARM design based processors and controllers all over. For instance we are utilizing ARM CORTEX processors in our mobiles, iPods and PCs as well as so forth.

Pi is a stunning instrument for acknowledging 'Web

of Things'. In this session we will talk about the equipment and programming necessities for Pi and setting up the Operating System for the main run of PI.

There are various sorts of Raspberry Pi sheets in the market now, with Raspberry Pi two Model B being the most mainstream. Raspberry Pi three Model B has likewise been propelled; it is practically like RPi 2, with some development include like on board Wi-Fi and Bluetooth availability, all the more dominant CPU and so on. We will talk about scarcely any qualities of "Raspberry Pi 2 B" presently.

Raspbeery Pi has four USB 2.0 ports. These ports can be associated with any USB gadgets, similar to mouse and console. With the main beginning itself, we need mouse and console, we will talk about it later. The four USB ports are demonstrated the figure.

Raspbeery Pi two has 1 Ethernet port. This port is for web network to the RASPBEERY PI two. This Ethernet port can likewise be utilized to move information among PI2 and your PC.

It has a 3.5mm jack port for associating earphones, if there should arise an occurrence of playing music from PI.

PI has a solitary HDMI port for associating a LCD/LED screen. The designs gave by the chip is genuinely great.

There is a smaller scale USB port on the board; we give capacity to the total board through this port. On the off chance that there are any changes in voltage gave at this port, the board won't work appropriately.

Rather than interfacing a Liquid Crystal Display screen we can associate a 3inch to 7inch touch show. We have inbuilt port for interfacing a touch show. We have a comparative port for interfacing a camera to the module; the camera module can be associated with PI with no extra connections.

There are (General Purpose Input Output) pins as well as a two control ground terminals. We can program there General Purpose Input Output pins for any utilization. Not many of pins likewise perform exceptional capacities, we will talk about them later.

Hardware Requirements:

1. Power supply - As said prior we self control the Raspberry Pi board by Micro USB port present on the board. Under ordinary activities the PI board needs a 5V, 1000mA (or 1A) control source. The voltage and current necessities are significant here. Any power source higher than 5V will harm the board for all time as well as for voltages lower than 4.8V, the load up won't work.

Here I am utilizing a 5V, 1000mA cell phone charger for controlling up my PI. Recall the base current rating for ordinary activity of PI board.

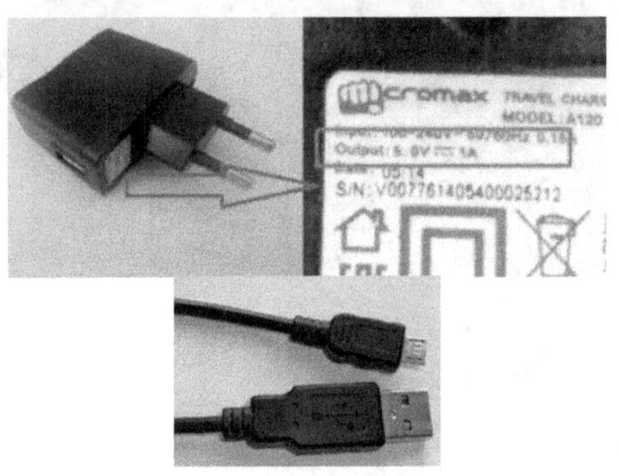

For interfacing the small scale Universal Serial Bus control, you need a decent quality link. In case you don't control the board from a decent USB link, regardless of what the power source, you will consistently have control deficiency on the board. You need a decent quality USB link as appeared in figure.

For higher tasks of PI, you need a power source which could convey in any event 2000mA or 2A. So in case you don't have a power wellspring of such kind, don't drive the PI by lower appraised control source, its better get another one.

Be that as it may, in case you have two connectors which can give every, you can interface one connector yield to the small scale USB, and the second one to the Universal Serial Bus 2.0 port, the two of them can share the heap. Here I have a 0.7A or 700mA connector which I interface with one of 4 USB ports on the chip.

2. You require a LCD or LED screen, you can utilize your old PC screen as a Raspberry Pi screen. Subsequent to picking your screen, you require to look whether the screen bolsters HDMI inputs or not. On the off chance that your screen has a HDMI port, at that point you simply need to get a male to male HDMI link as appeared in figure.

On the off chance that your screen doesn't bolster HDMI like mine, at that point your screen must have VGA support as appeared in figure. You need a High-Definition Multimedia Interface to Video Graphics Array converter; you can purchase this at any electronic store. This gadget changes over HDMI from PI to VGA yield. So we can interface a Video Graphics Array screen to a PI. The gadget is appeared in figure.

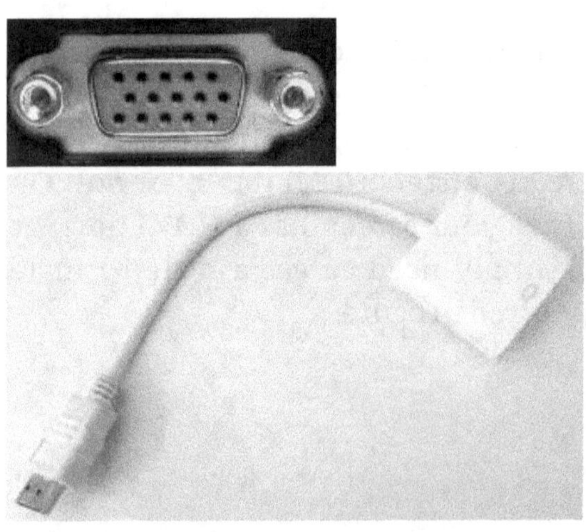

3.You need a Mouse as well as Keyboard, ensure they are USB driven sort or you won't have the option to interface it to PI, since PI just has USB ports.

4. You need a Micro Secure Digital card (Memory card) and a Secure Digital Card Reader (or Adapter) to associate SD card to PC (or workstation). The SD card must be of 8GB or higher. If not, you won't have the option to introduce the OS (Operating System) on to the PI effectively. And furthermore the Class of SD card should be equivalent or higher than 4, for better speed. "Speed Class" speaks to the composing speed like class 10 methods 10 MB/second.

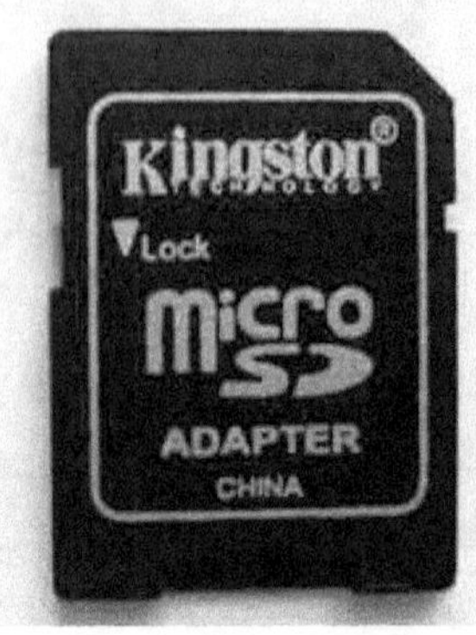

Presently we have all the essential Hardwares, need to Getting Initiated with Raspberry Pi, and we will currently examine the Software Requirement.

Software Requirements:

First we need the OS (Operating System) for the PI, which can be downloaded from Downloads segment of Raspberry Pi site:

https://www.raspberrypi.org/downloads/

It will give all of you the supporting OS for the RASP-BEERY PI 2. You can download and introduce any OS on Pi which is recorded there. We will download official upheld Operating System for Raspberry Pi, which is "Raspbian". Snap on "RASPBIAN", and download the Full work area picture of Raspbian Jessie. Concentrate the Rasbian picture from the Zip document, utilizing any Zip record extractor like Winrar or Winzip.

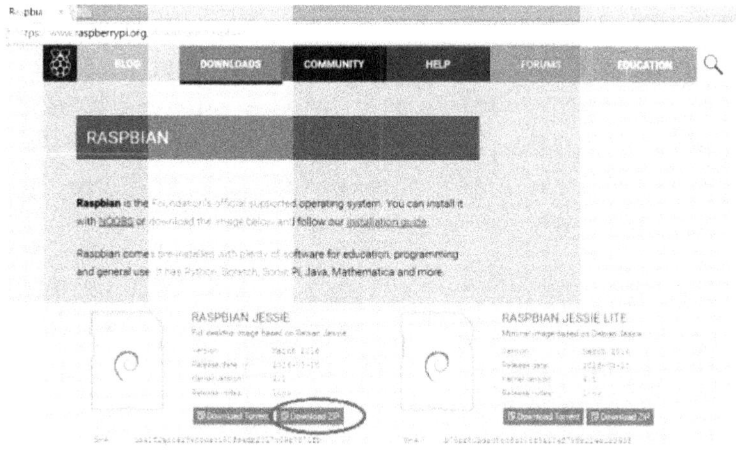

We likewise need an Image essayist programming for introducing the OS on to the Micro Secure Digital card. We have utilized "win32diskimager" to compose the picture on Micro SD card, which can be downloaded from underneath connect:

https://sourceforge.net/ventures/win32diskimager/

Once the download finishes, introduce the product, you will see a symbol on the Desktop Screen after establishment.

Get started with Raspberry Pi: Steps

Presently, we have all the product and hard product required to begin with the RASPBEERY PI 2.

To introduce OS on to a SD card pursue beneath steps:

1. Unfasten the 'Raspbian Jessie' (OS ZIP document we

downloaded from raspberry site) on to the work area; you will see an Image symbol upon extraction on the screen as demonstrated as follows. Ensure you have at any rate 5 GB free circle space on 'C' drive of your PC. The extraction document size would be more prominent than 3GB.

2. Supplement the SD card into the USB card peruser or Card Adapter. Attachment the card peruser to the Personal Computers. You should consider the to be on the screen as demonstrated as follows.

3. Arrangement the card drive by Right snap on it and select Format. Select File framework as 'FAT 32' and tick on 'Speedy Format'. At long last snap on 'Start' catch to Format the drive.

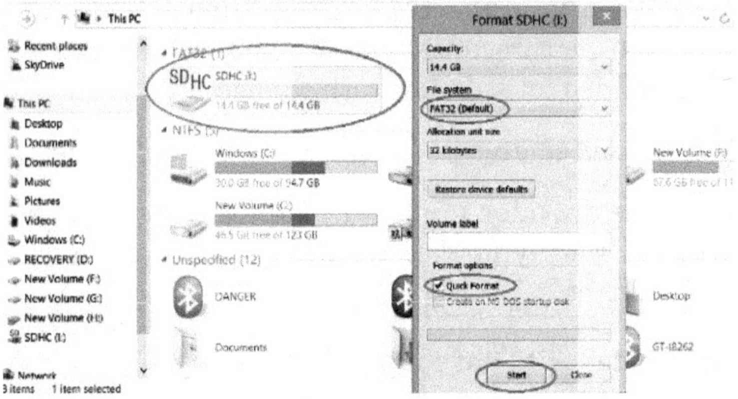

4. Subsequent to organizing, run the "win32disk-imager" application, which we have downloaded as clarified beforehand.

5. Pick the SD card drive, peruse for the Raspbian OS

picture record (which is removed on the screen) and Click on 'Compose' symbol, to begin composing the separated OS document on to the SD card. This is appeared in underneath figure.

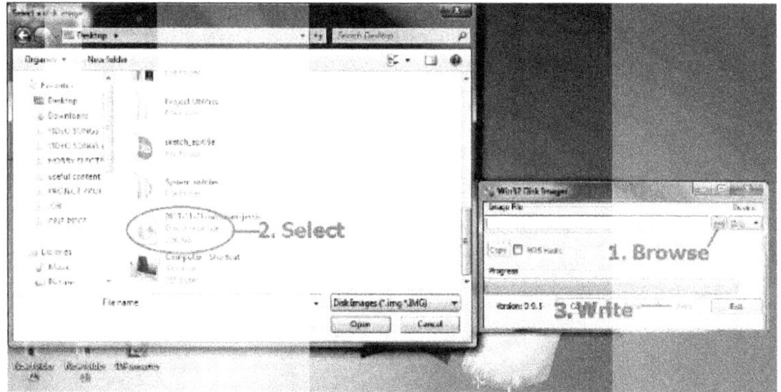

6. After consummation of composing, securely expel the SD card from the peruser.

Presently we have SD card with Raspbian OS introduced on it and having all the gear required to Get Started with Raspberry PI 2. In the following session we will have the primary take a gander at the "PI" OS and we will discuss designing the BIOS of Raspberry Pi.

14. PROGRAMMED LIGHT FENCE CIRCUIT WITH ALARM

Light fence circuit is utilized to recognize the nearness of any human or item in a specific region. The recognizing scope of Light Fence Circuit is about 1.5 to 3 meters. It's very easy to structure the circuit utilizing LDR and Op-amp. This compact circuit can work easily with an ordinarily accessible 9V battery and the alert sound created from the ringer is sufficiently uproarious to distinguish the nearness of a human, vehicle or item.

This sort of security framework can likewise worked by utilizing different sensors as opposed to utilizing LDR, as:

- PIR based Burglar Alarm Circuit

- IR Based Security Alarm

- Laser Security Alarm Circuit

- Attractive Door Alarm Circuit utilizing Hall Sensor

Components Required

- LM741 Op-amp IC
- BC557 – PNP Transistor
- 555 timer IC
- LDR
- Resistor (210, 1K, 5.7K, 100k, 1M)
- Capacitor (0.1uf, 10uf)
- Potentiometer – 100K
- Buzzer
- LED
- Battery - 9V
- Breadboard

LDR

LDRs are produced using semiconductor materials to empower them to have their light-touchy properties. There are numerous sorts however one material is mainstream and it is cadmium sulfide. These LDRs or PHOTO RESISTORS chips away at the guideline of "Photograph Conductivity". Presently what this rule says is, at whatever point light falls on the outside of the LDR (for this situation) the conductance of the component increments or at the end of the day, the opposition of the Light Dependent Resistor falls when the light falls on the outside of the Light Dependent Resistor. This property of the diminishing in obstruction for the LDR is accomplished in light in case it is a property of semiconductor material utilized superficially.

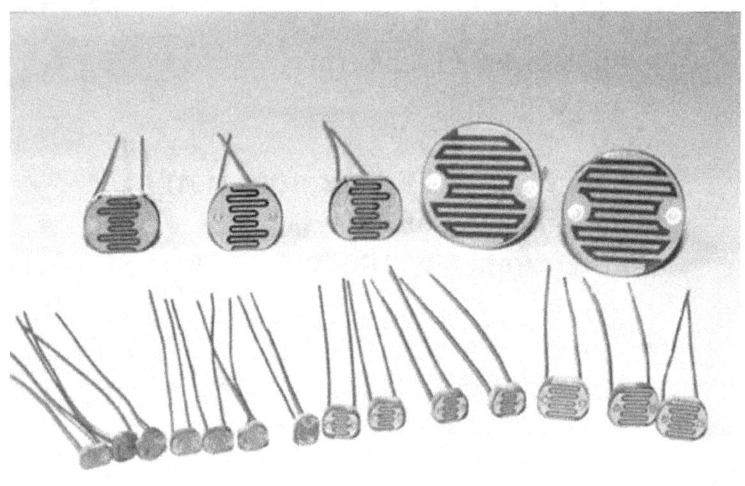

We have recently manufactured made numerous Circuits utilizing LDR, which use LDR to robotize the lights as indicated by necessity.

555 Timer IC

555 Timer IC is one of the most utilized IC in gadgets, particularly for activating reason. To become familiar with it pursue our different 555 Timer circuits.

Here we are utilizing 555 Timer IC in astable mode to make a blaring sound with Buzzer. Beneath we have clarified the conduct of every one of the pin of 555 Timer IC while working in Astable mode.

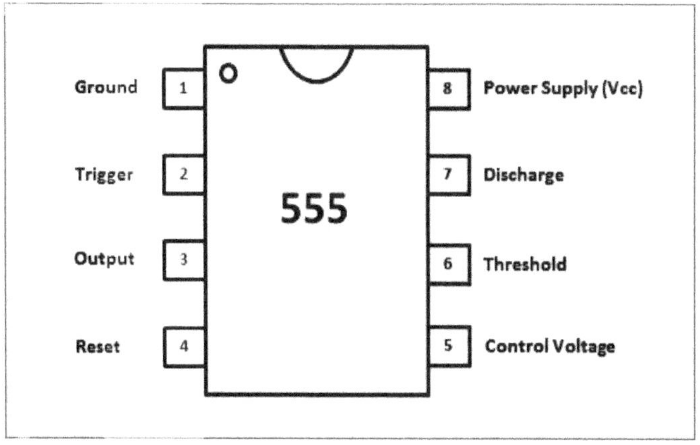

Pin 1. Ground: This pin ought to be associated with ground.

Pin 2. TRIGGER: Trigger pin is hauled from the negative contribution of comparator two. The Lower comparator yield is associated with SET pin of flip-flop. A -ve heartbeat (< Vcc/3) on this Pin sets the Flip failure and yield goes High.

Pin 3. Yield: This pin likewise has no exceptional capacity. This is yield pin where Load is associated. It very well may be utilized as source or sink and drive upto 200mA current.

Pin 4. Reset: There is a flip-flop in the clock chip. Reset pin is legitimately associated with MR (Master Reset) of the flip-flop. This is a functioning Low pin and typically associated with VCC for anticipating inadvertent Reset.

Pin 5. Control Pin: The control pin is associated from the -ve information pin of comparator one. Yield Pulse width can be constrained by applying voltage at this Pin, regardless of RC organize. Ordinarily this pin is pulled down with a capacitor (0.01uF), to maintain a strategic distance from undesirable clamor obstruction with the working.

Pin 6. Limit: Threshold pin voltage decides when to reset the flip-flop in the clock. The edge pin is drawn from positive contribution of upper comparator. On the off chance that the control pin is open, at that point a voltage equivalent to or more noteworthy than VCC*(2/3) will reset the flip-flop. So the yield goes low.

Pin 7. Release: This pin is drawn from the open authority of transistor. Since the transistor (on which release pin got taken, Q1) got its base associated with Qbar. At whatever point the yield goes low or the flip-flop gets reset, the release pin is dismantled to ground and capacitor releases.

Pin 8. Power or VCC: It is associated with positive voltage (+3.6v to +15v).

Circuit Diagram

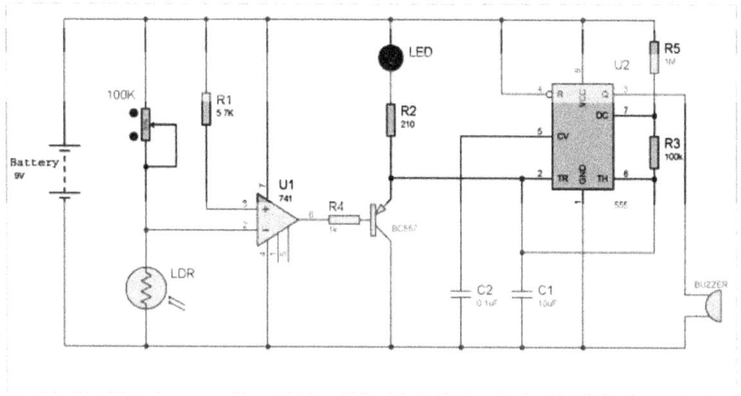

Complete circuit graph for Automatic Fence Lighting with Alarm is appeared previously. LDR is put looking towards the passage and a potentiometer is utilized to change the affectability of the gadget. You can likewise include a switch between the negative pin of the battery and LDR's grounded pin to control this security framework physically.

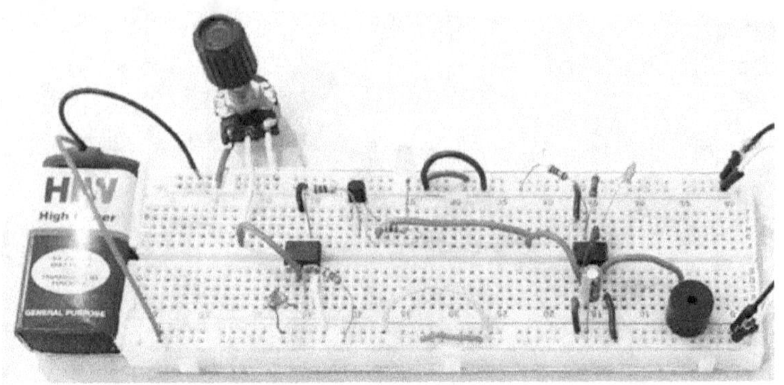

Working of Light Fence Circuit

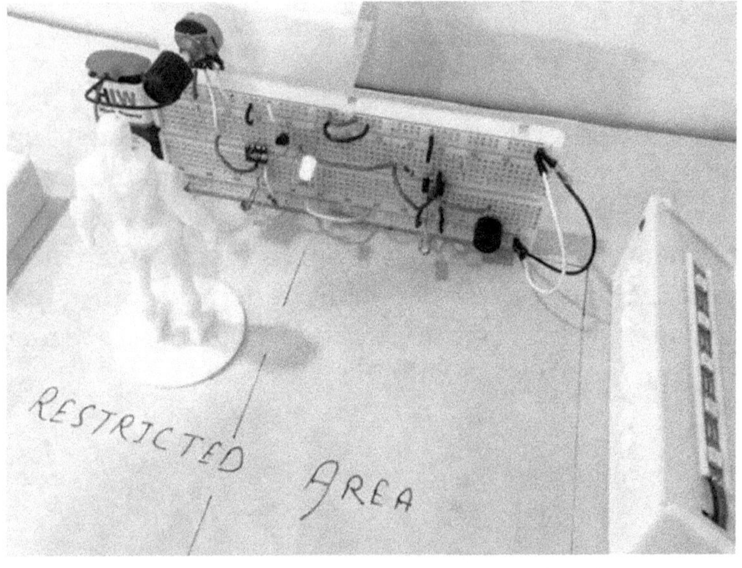

Here, the operation amp IC is utilized as a voltage comparator and the 555 clock IC is set in an astable mode. The LDR and the potentiometer are making a voltage divider circuit. The yield of this divider circuit will change as indicated by the power of light falls on the Light Dependent Resistor. The divider is associated with the upsetting pin of the Op-amp IC. The non-rearranging pin is associated with supply through a 5.7Kohm resistor, so the voltage esteem at the non-modifying is fix. You can supplant this resistor with a 10K potentiometer to change the voltage according to the prerequisite.

We can change the affectability of the gadget by utilizing the potentiometer VR1 associated in arrangement with the LDR. At the point when the voltage at non-reversing input is more noteworthy than or equivalent to the reference voltage the yield (at pin 6) of the operation amp IC yield (PIN 6) goes HIGH. Become familiar with working of operation amp by following the different operation amp based circuits.

As indicated by the circuit chart, when LDR distinguishes any movement the yield of the Op-amp IC goes LOW, and PNP transistor T1 start leading. Consequently, the LED beginnings shining and the 555 clock IC get activated. Here, 555 clock IC is in Astable mode and a preset time delay is given by R3, R5 and C1.

So at whatever point some individual or item enters in restricted territory, his shadows will be detected by the LDR and the circuit triggers the caution.

15. CAPACITOR ESR METER UTILIZING OSCILLOSCOPE

Capacitors appear to be all fine till you arrive at where a power supply comes up short or won't perform ideally. Also, if the issue is clamor, there is a basic fix, you simply include more capacitors. However, that doesn't fathom it. What could not be right?

The issue emerges from the guileless suspicion that capacitors (to a huge degree) are 'perfect' gadgets, while indeed, they are definitely not. Those undesired impacts are a result of something many refer to as inner obstruction or Equivalent Series Resistance (ESR). Capacitors have a limited inner obstruction as a result of the materials utilized in their development. We have clarified ESR and ESL in capacitors in subtleties in past article.

Various kinds of capacitors have diverse ESR ranges. For instance, electrolytic capacitors when all is said in done have higher Equivalent Series Resistances than clay capacitors. For some applications, it gets imperative to quantify the inner opposition of capacitors. Also, today in this article we will fabricate an ESR Meter and figure out how to quantify the ESR of capacitor utilizing 555 Timer IC and Transistors.

Capacitor ESR Measurement

At the starting ESR Measurement may arise to be a simple assignment.

Obstruction can without much of a stretch be controlled by applying a steady present and estimating the voltage drop over the Device under testing.

Consider the possibility that we apply a consistent current to a capacitor. The voltage rises straightly and settles at a worth dictated by the stockpile voltage, which (for our motivations) is futile.

Now the time has come to return to something we learnt in school-"Capacitors square DC and pass AC"

In the wake of making a couple improving ends, we comprehend that capacitors are essentially a short out at high frequencies as well as the capacitive part is 'shorted out' of the circuit as well as the entirety of the voltage is dropped over the interior opposition.

The upside of this strategy is that we don't have to know the current in the event that we know the interior opposition of the sign source being utilized, in light in case now the ESR and inward obstruction (of the source) structure a voltage divider, the proportion of protections is the proportion of the voltage drops, as well as realizing three we can without much of a stretch decide the other one.

An oscilloscope is utilized to quantify the waveforms at the info and at the capacitor.

Parts List

For the Oscillator:

1. 555 clock – both CMOS and bipolar will work fine, however CMOS is prescribed for high frequencies

2. 100K potentiometer – utilized for recurrence tuning

3. 1nF capacitor – timing

4. 10uF artistic capacitor - decoupling

The Power Stage:

1. BC548 NPN bipolar transistor

2. BC558 PNP bipolar transistor

A snappy note about the selection of transistors - any

little sign transistor with a high addition (300 and upwards) and a to some degree huge current (50mA +) will work fine.

3. 560? base resistor

4. 47? yield resistor – this can be anything from 10? to 100?.

Circuit Diagram

The following is the circuit chart for this ESR Capacitor Tester circuit-

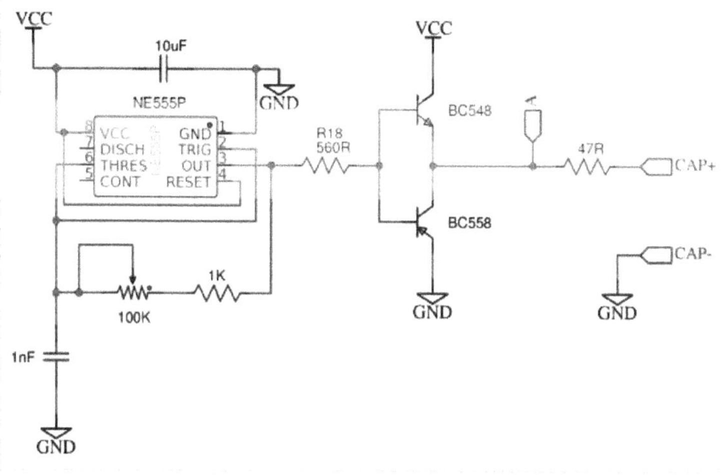

This ESR Meter Circuit can be separated into two areas, the 555 clock and the yield arrange.

1. The 555 Oscillator:

The 555 circuit is a regular astable multivibrator that puts out a square wave with a recurrence of a couple hundred kilohertz. At this recurrence, practically all capacitors demonstration like a short. The 100K pot permits recurrence tuning to get the most reduced conceivable voltage over the top.

2. The Power Stage:

This is a workaround to another issue. We could straightforwardly interface the capacitor to the yield of the 555 clock, yet then we would need to know the yield impedance precisely.

To wipe out this, a push-pull yield arrange with an arrangement resistor is utilized. The resistor gives the yield impedance.

Here is the how the total equipment of this Equivalent Series Resistance Meter circuit looks:

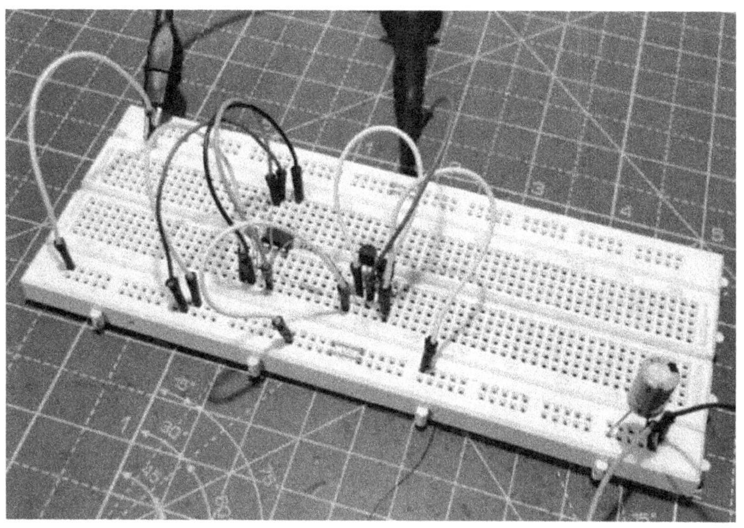

Calculating ESR of Capacitor

From the voltage divider condition, we infer the accompanying recipe:

$$ESR = (V_{CAP} \cdot R_{OUTPUT}) / (V_{OUTPUT} - V_{CAP})$$

Where ESR is the interior obstruction of the capacitor, VCAP is the sign over the capacitor (estimated at hub CAP+), ROUTPUT is the yield opposition of the power organize (here, 47 Ohms) and VOUTPUT is the yield signal voltage as estimated at point An in the circuit.

While utilizing this circuit it is prescribed to set the

extension test to 1X to expand the affectability and diminishing the transfer speed to dispose of a portion of the clamor so as to make an exact estimation.

To start with, the top to top voltage is estimated at point An, in front of the impedance and noted. At that point the capacitor is connected. Zoom in till you see a square wave. Fidget the pot till the waveform doesn't turn out to be any littler.

Contingent upon the sort of capacitor, the top to top voltage of the subsequent waveform ought to be in the request for a couple tens or many millivolts.

Example: Measuring ESR for a 100uf Electrolytic Capacitor

Here is the crude yield waveform of the power organize:

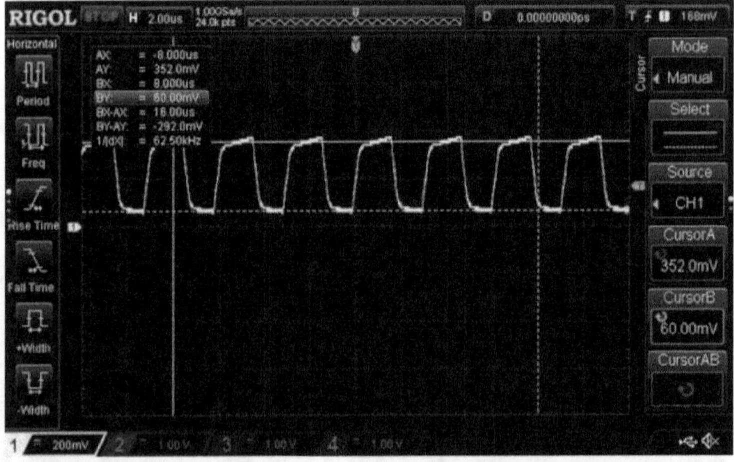

Power Stage Output Waveform

Furthermore, here is the voltage at the capacitor. Note all the commotion superimposed on the sign – be cautious with the estimation.

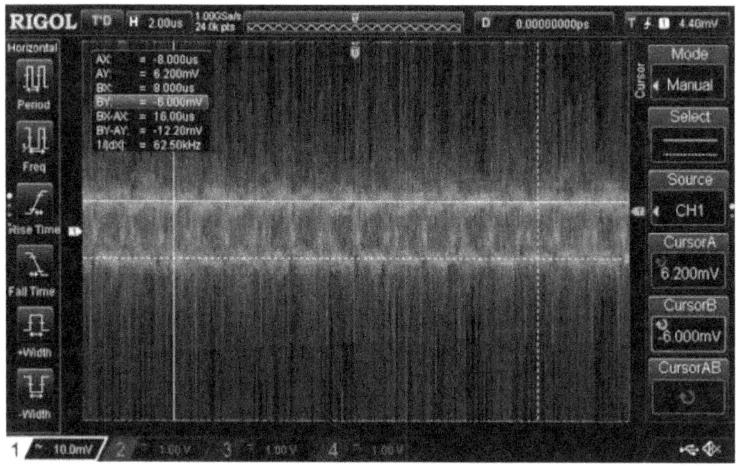

Voltage across the Capacitor

Connecting the qualities into the equation, we get an ESR of 198m?.

Capacitor's ESR is a significant parameter when structuring power circuits and here we manufactured a basic ESR estimating gadget dependent on the 555 clock.

16. CHARGE PUMP CIRCUIT - GETTING HIGHER VOLTAGE FROM LOW VOLTAGE SOURCE

The circumstance is straightforward – you have a low voltage supply rail, say 3.3V, and you require to control something that requirements 5V. This is an extreme call, particularly if batteries are included. The main evident way is a switch mode converter, all the more explicitly a lift converter.

This is the place we hit a barricade – support converters are wasteful at low powers, since a great deal of vitality is devoured only for keeping the guideline on point and driving the power switch. Likewise, switch mode converters of this sort are uproarious – this is an issue in case you're managing touchy hardware. You're in the awkward situation of an overbuilt arrangement. Straight controllers don't work backward, with the goal that's precluded as under-designed.

So where do we adhere to a meaningful boundary between over-designed and under-built?

The response to this issue is simply the Charge Pump – which is a sort of switch mode control supply. As the name recommends, this sort of converter moves discrete charges around and the part that stores these discrete charges is the capacitor, so this sort of converter is additionally called the Flying Capacitor Converter.
A charge siphon makes discrete products of the info voltage utilizing capacitors.

How does a Charge Pump Work?

The most ideal approach to comprehend this is to envision the accompanying circumstance.

You charge a capacitor utilizing a nine V battery, so the voltage over the capacitor is likewise 9V. At that point you take another capacitor as well as energize it to 9V as well. Presently associate the two capacitors in arrangement, and measure the voltage crosswise over them – 18V.

This is the fundamental rule of activity of the charge siphon – take two capacitors, charge them independently and afterward put them in arrangement, however in a genuine charge siphon the improving is done electronically.

Obviously this isn't constrained to only two capacitors, progressive stages can be fell to acquire higher voltages on the yield.

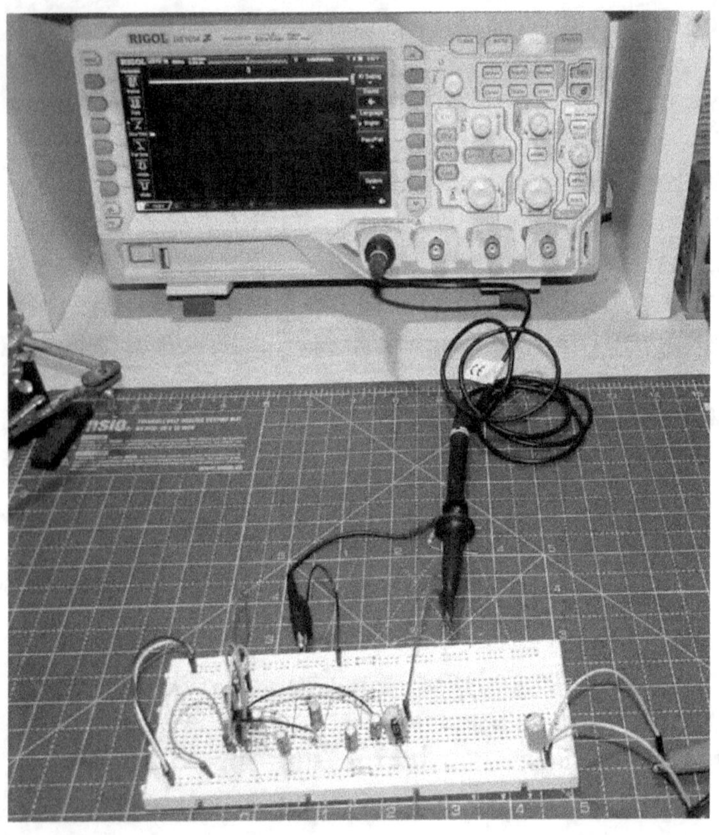

Limitations of Charge Pumps

Before we manufacture one, it is a smart thought to become more acquainted with the confinements of charge siphons.

1. Accessible yield current – since charge siphons are only capacitors that are charged and released in cycles, the accessible current is low – there are uncommon situations where utilizing the correct chip can get you 100mA, yet at low efficiencies.

2. The more stages you include doesn't imply that the voltage yield builds that multiple occasions – each stage stacks the yield of the past stage, so the yield is certainly not an ideal numerous of the info. This issue deteriorates the more stages you include.

Building a Charge Pump Circuit

The circuit appeared here is for a basic three phase charge siphon that uses the evergreen 555 clock IC. It could be said, this circuit is 'particular' – stages can be fell to expand the yield voltage (in view of impediment number two).

Parts Required

1. For the 555 Oscillator

- 555 clock – bipolar variation

- 10uF electrolytic capacitor (decoupling)

- 2x 100nF earthenware capacitor (decoupling)

- 100pF earthenware capacitor (timing)

- 1K resistor (timing)

- 10K resistor (timing)

2. For the Charge Pump

- 6x IN4148 diodes (UF4007 additionally suggested)

- 5x 10uF electrolytic capacitors

- 100uF electrolytic capacitor

Something critical to note is that every one of the capacitors utilized in the charge siphon must be evaluated for a couple of volts more than the normal yield voltage.

Circuit Diagram

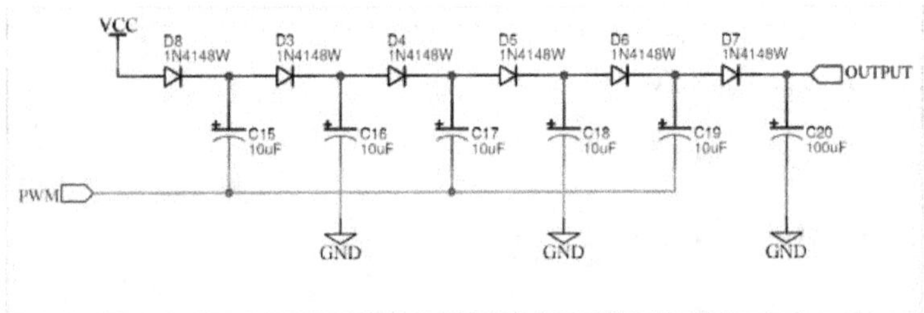

This is what it looks like on breadboard:

Charge Pump Circuit Description

1. The 555 Timer

The circuit appeared here is a direct 555 clock astable oscillator. The planning segments bring about a recurrence of around 500kHz (which for a bipolar 555 is an accomplishment in itself). This high recurrence guarantees that the capacitors on the charge siphon are 'invigorated' intermittently with the goal that the voltage on the yield doesn't have a lot of wave.

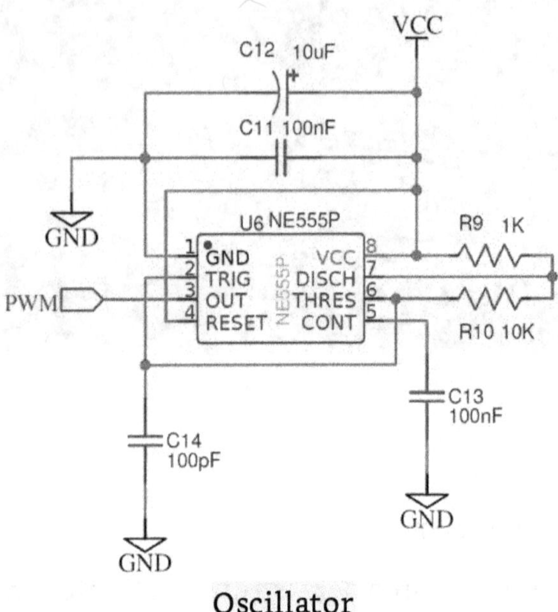

Oscillator

2. The Charge Pump

This is the most scary piece of the entire circuit. Like most different things it tends to be comprehended by separating it to a solitary unit:

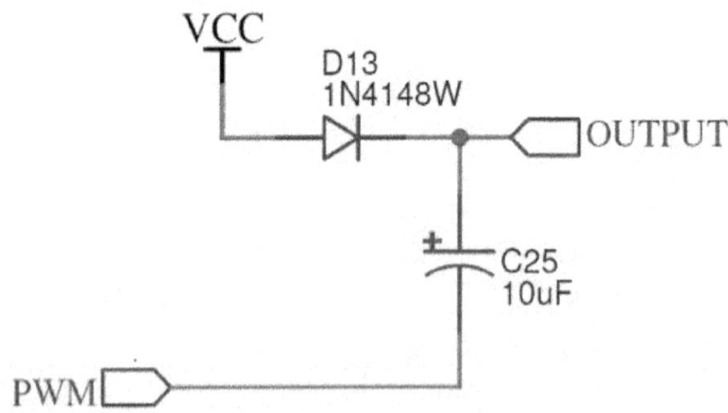

Single Stage

How about we accept that pin 3, the yield of the 555 clock, is low during startup. This outcomes in the capacitor charging through the diode since the negative terminal is currently grounded. At the point when the yield goes high, the negative pin goes high as well – however since there's as of now a charge on the capacitor (that can't go anyplace as a result of the diode) the voltage seen at the positive terminal of the capacitor is adequately twofold the info voltage.

Here's the +ve terminal of the capacitor:

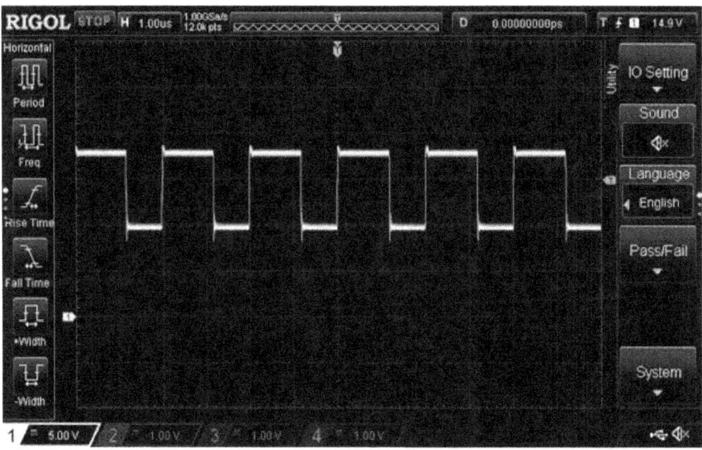

The conclusive outcome is that you're successfully adding a counterbalanced of VCC to the yield of the

555 clock.

Presently this voltage straightforwardly as a yield is pointless, since there's a gigantic half wave. To settle this, we include a pinnacle finder as appeared in underneath figure:

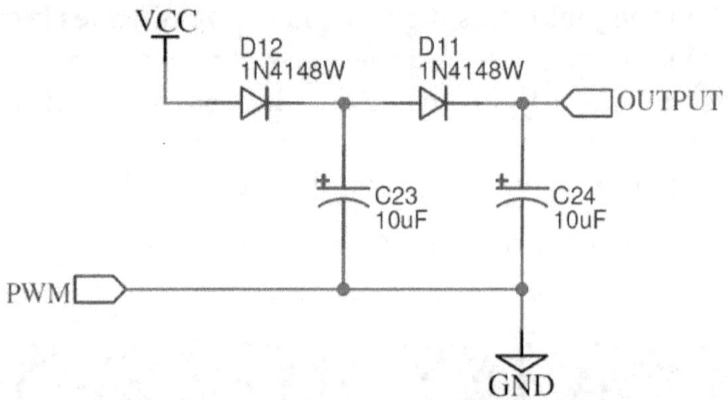

Single Stage with Peak Detector

This is the yield of above circuit:

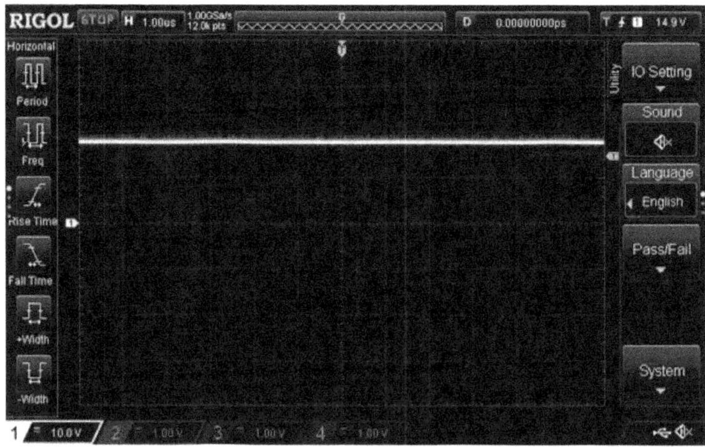

Also, we've effectively multiplied the voltage yield!

Circuit Construction Tips

The bipolar 555 is known for the inventory spikes it creates on the stockpile rail, since the yield push-pull arrange practically short the inventory during changes. So decoupling is required.

I'll take a snappy temporary re-route to disclose to you something about legitimate decoupling.

Here's the VCC pin of the oscillator with no decoupling:

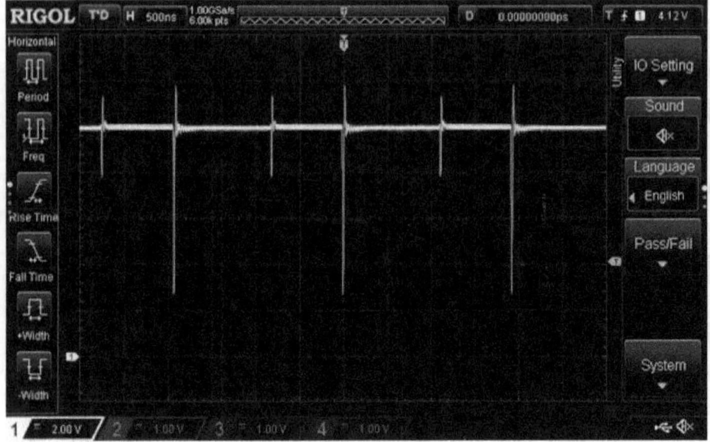

Also, here's a similar pin with legitimate decoupling:

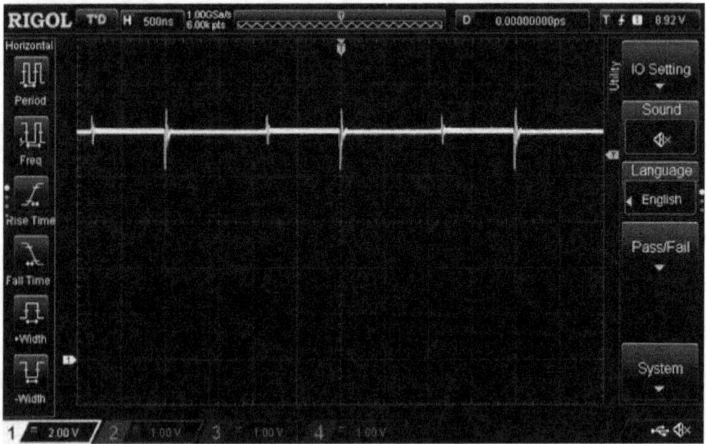

You can plainly observe the distinction a tad of decoupling makes.

Low inductance fired SMD capacitors are prescribed for the charge siphon arrange. Schottky diodes with a low forward voltage drop likewise improve execution.

Utilizing a CMOS 555 with an appropriate yield organize (possibly a door driver like the TC4420) can decrease (yet not kill) the stockpile spikes.

Charge Pump Variations

Charge siphons not just build voltage, they can be utilized to reverse voltage extremity.

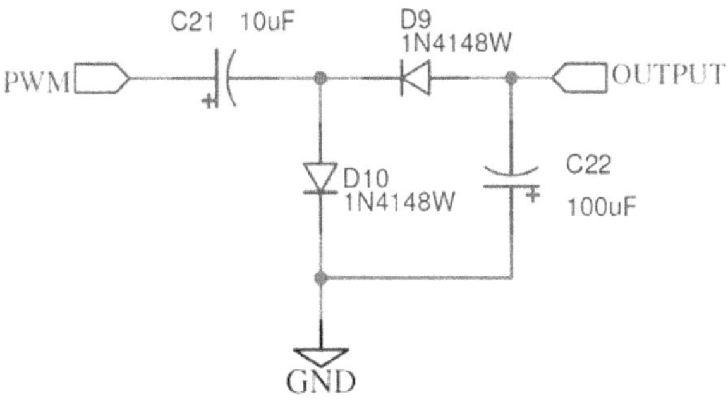

Inverter

This circuit works a similar route as the voltage doubler – when the 555 yield goes high, the top energizes, and when the yield goes low charge is pulled during that time capacitor in the turn around heading, making a negative voltage on the yield.

Where do I use a Charge Pump?

- Bipolarity supply for operation amps in a circuit where just a solitary voltage is accessible. Operation amps don't expend more current so this is an ideal fit. The decent thing about this is an inverter and a doubler can be driven from a similar yield, making, state, ±12V supply from a 5V supply.

- Entryway drivers – bootstrapping is a choice however a charge siphon can possibly produce higher voltage, state, having a 12V door drive from a 3.3V stockpile. Bootstrapping wouldn't give you more than seven V for this situation.

So Charge siphons are straightforward and effective gadgets used to make discrete products of the information voltage.

❖ ❖ ❖

17. BASIC CURVE TRACER CIRCUIT: TRACING THE CURVE FOR RESISTOR, DIODE AND TRANSISTOR

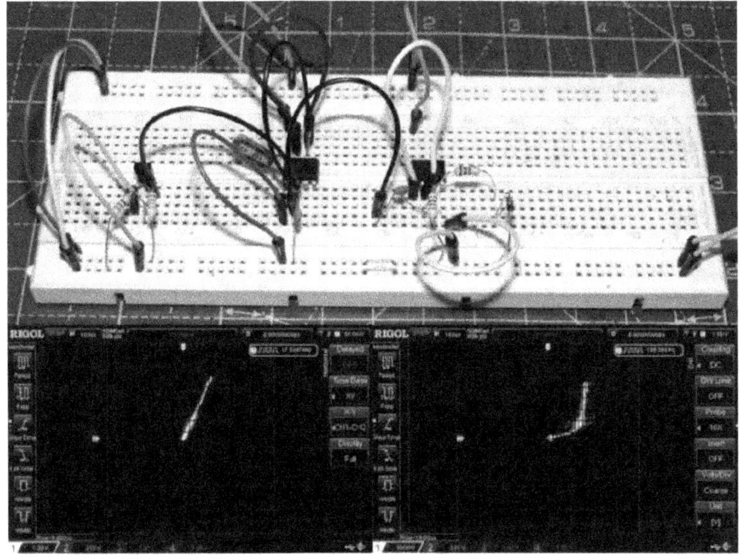

Simple Curve Tracer Circuit

A large portion of hardware manages Tracing Curves, be it the trademark move bend for a criticism circle, a resistor's straight VI line or a transistor's authority voltage versus current bend.

These bends give us an instinctive comprehension of how a gadget acts in a circuit. A scientific methodology may include connecting discrete voltage and current qualities into a numerical recipe and diagramming the outcomes, usually with the x hub speaking to voltage and the y hub speaking to current.

This methodology works, however some of the time it is dull. What's more, as each gadgets specialist knows, the conduct of segments, all things considered, can differ (regularly generally) from the recipe depicting its activity.

Here we will utilize a circuit (Sawtooth waveform) to apply discrete expanding voltage to the part whose VI bend we require to draw and afterward utilize an Oscilloscope to see the outcomes.

Simple Curve Tracer

To plot a bend progressively we have to apply progressive discrete voltage esteems to our gadget under test, so how it very well may be finished?

The answer for our concern is the Sawtooth Waveform.

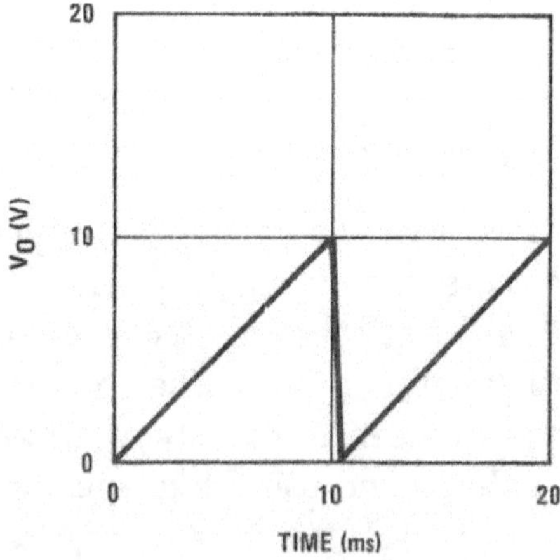

Sawtooth Waveform

The Sawtooth waveform rises directly and returns to zero occasionally. This permits utilization of a ceaselessly expanding voltage on the gadget under test and delivers a persistent follow on a chart (for this situation the oscilloscope).

An oscilloscope in the XY mode is utilized to 'read' the circuit. The X pivot is combined with the gadget under test and the Y hub is combined with the Sawtooth waveform.

The circuit utilized here is a straightforward variety of a bend tracer utilizing normal parts like the 555 clock and the LM358 operation amp.

Components Required

1. For the Timer

- 555 clock – any variation

- 100nF earthenware capacitor (decoupling)

- 10uF electrolytic capacitor (decoupling)

- 1K resistor (current source)

- 10uF electrolytic capacitor (timing)

- BC557 PNP transistor generally identical

- 10K resistor (current source)

2. For the Op-amp Amplifier

- LM358 generally practically identical opamp

- 10uF electrolytic capacitor (decoupling)

- 10nF earthenware capacitor (AC coupling)

- 10M resistor (AC coupling)

- Test resistor (relies upon gadget under test, for the many part between 50 Ohms just as a couple hundred Ohms.)

Circuit Diagram

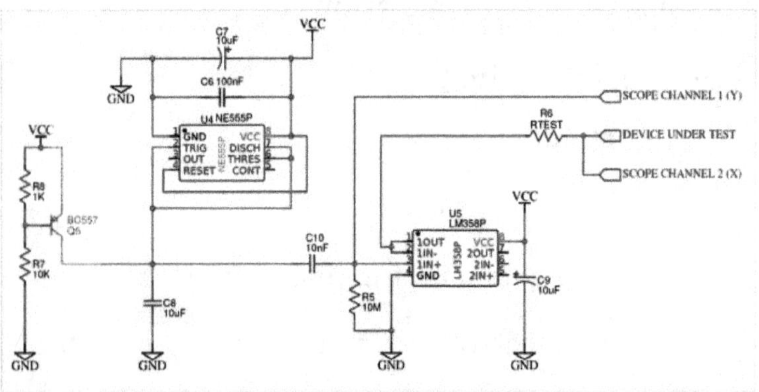

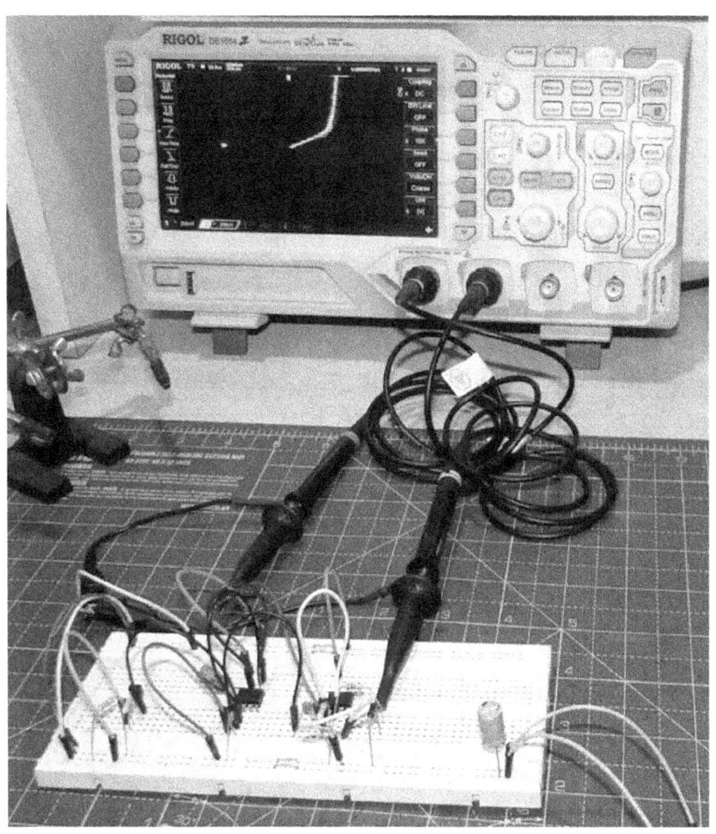

Working Explanation

1. The 555 Timer

The circuit utilized here is a basic variety of the exemplary 555 astable circuit which will function as Sawtooth waveform generator.

Generally the planning resistor is bolstered through a resistor associated with the power supply, yet here it is associated with an (unrefined) consistent current source.

The steady current stock works by giving a fixed base-producer inclination voltage, bringing about a (to some degree) consistent authority current. Charging a capacitor utilizing a consistent current outcomes in a straight incline waveform.

This design gets the yield legitimately from the capacitor yield (which is the sawtooth incline we're searching for) and not from pin 3, which gives thin negative heartbeats here.

This circuit is shrewd as in it utilizes the 555's interior system to control a consistent current source-capacitor slope generator.

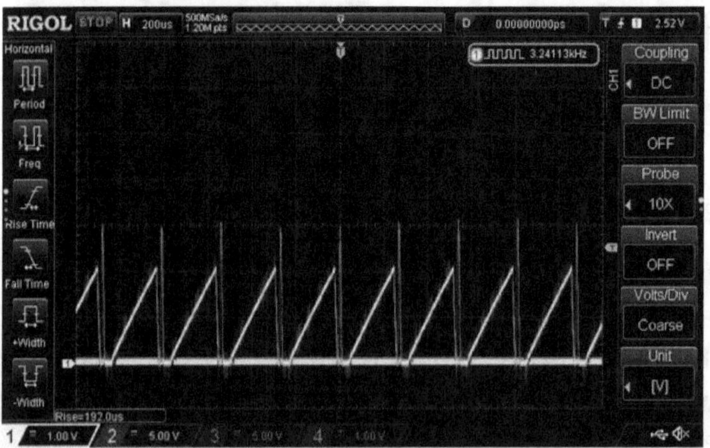

A Crude Sawtooth Waveform – But Adequate

2. The Amplifier

Since the yield is gotten legitimately from the capacitor (which is charged from the present source), the current accessible to control the gadget under test (DUT) is basically zero.

To fix this, we're utilizing the great LM358 opamp as a voltage (and along these lines current) cradle. This to some degree expands the current accessible to the DUT.

The capacitor Sawtooth waveform sways between 1/3 and 2/3 Vcc (555 activity), which is unusable in a bend tracer since the voltage doesn't incline from zero giving a 'deficient' follow. To fix this the contribution from the 555 is AC coupled to the cushion input.

The 10M resistor is a touch of dark enchantment – it was discovered during testing that if the resistor was not included, the yield essentially drifted to Vcc and remained there! This is a result of the parasitic information capacitance – alongside the high info impedance, it frames an integrator! The 10M resistor is sufficient to release this parasitic capacitance yet insufficient to altogether stack the steady current circuit.

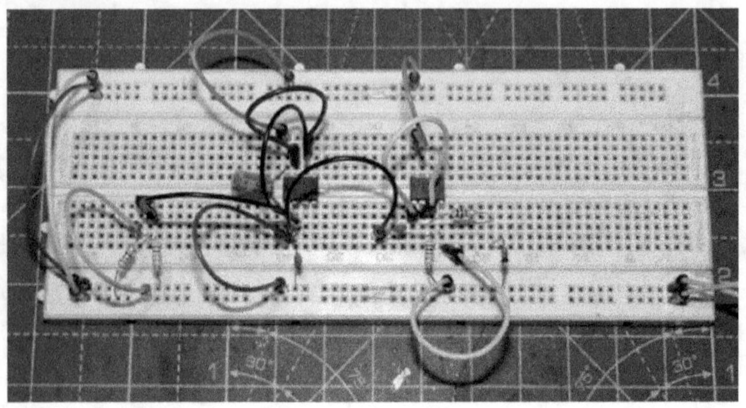

How to improve the Curve Tracing Results

Since this circuit includes high frequencies and high impedances, cautious development is expected to avoid undesirable commotion and swaying.

Abundant decoupling is prescribed. Beyond what many would consider possible, attempt to abstain from breadboarding this circuit and utilize a PCB or a perfboard.

This circuit is rough and henceforth unstable. It is prescribed to control this circuit from a variable voltage source. Indeed, even a LM317 will work when absolutely necessary. This circuit is generally steady at around 7.5V.

Another significant interesting point is the flat scale setting on the extension – in the event that excessively high, at that point all the low recurrence clamor makes the follow fluffy and on the off chance that excessively low, at that point there's insufficient information to get a 'total' follow. Once more, this relies upon the power supply setting.

Getting a useable follow requires cautious tuning of the oscilloscope timebase setting and information voltage.

On the off chance that you need valuable estimations, at that point a test resistor and the information on opamp yield qualities is required. With a little math great qualities can be gotten.

How to use Curve Tracer Circuit

There are two basic things to remember – the X pivot speaks to the voltage and the Y hub speaks to the current.

On an oscilloscope, examining the X pivot is very straightforward – the voltage is 'as seems to be', for example compares to the volts per division set on the oscilloscope.

The Y or current pivot is marginally trickier. We're not legitimately estimating the current here, rather we're estimating the voltage dropped over the test resistor because of the current across the circuit.

It is sufficient on the off chance that we measure the pinnacle voltage esteem on the Y pivot. For this situation, it's 2V, as observed in past figure.
So the pinnacle current through the test circuit is

$$I_{sweep} = V_{peak}/R_{test}.$$

This speaks to the 'clear' current range, from 0 - Isweep.

Contingent upon the setting, the diagram can stretch out into the same number of divisions on the screen as that accessible. So the current per division is just the pinnacle current partitioned by the quantity of divisions the diagram reaches out to, as it were the line //el to the X hub where the top 'tip' of the chart contacts.

Curve Tracing for Diode

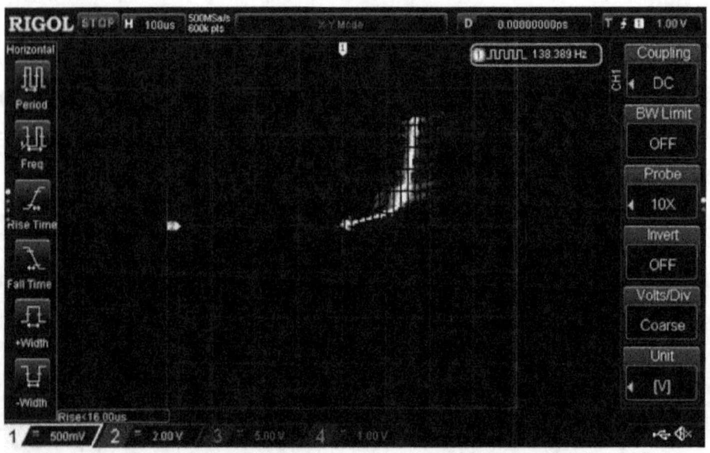

Diode VI Characteristic Curve

All the clamor and fluff depicted above is seen here.

Be that as it may, the diode bend can unmistakably be seen, with the 'knee' point at 0.7V (note the 500mV / division X scale).

Note that the X hub relates precisely with the normal 0.7V, which legitimizes the 'as is' temperament of the X pivot perusing.

The test obstruction utilized here was 1K, so the present range was from 0mA – 2mA. Here the diagram doesn't surpass two divisions (around), so an unpleasant scale would be 1mA/division.

Curve Tracing for Resistor

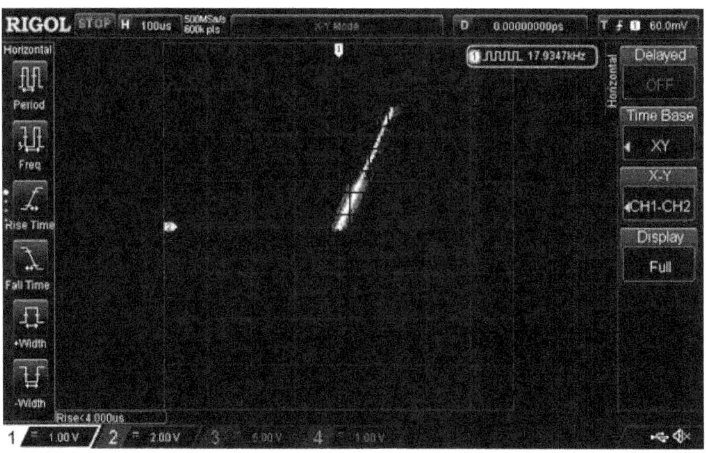

Resistor VI Characteristic Curve

Resistors are electrically the least difficult gadgets,

with a straight VI bend, a.k.a Ohm's law, R = V/I. Clearly low worth resistors have soak inclines (higher I for given V) and high worth resistors have progressively delicate slants (less I for given V).

The test opposition here was 100 Ohms, so the present range was 0mA – 20mA. Since the chart stretches out to 2.5 divisions, the current per division is 8mA.

The present ascents 16mA for a volt, so the opposition is 1V/16mA = 62 Ohms, which is proper since a 100 Ohm pot was the DUT.

Curve Tracing for Transistor

Since the transistor is a three terminal gadget, the quantity of estimations that can be made is very huge, nonetheless, just a couple of those estimations discover basic use, one of them being the reliance of authority voltage on base current (both referenced to ground, obviously) at a steady gatherer current.

Utilizing our bend tracer this ought to be a simple errand. The base is snared to a consistent inclination and the X pivot to the authority. The test opposition gives the 'steady' current.

The resultant follow should look like this:

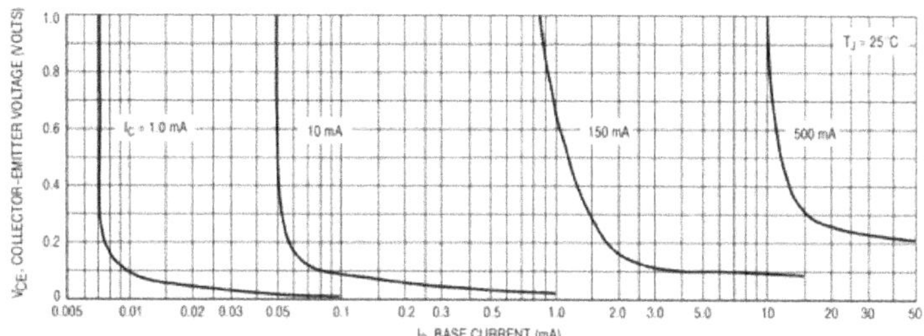

I_B Vs V_{CE}

Note that the chart appeared above is a log scale, recollect that the oscilloscope is straight naturally.

So Curve tracers are gadgets that produce VI follows for basic segments and help increase a natural comprehension of segment qualities.

18.
STRAIGHTFOR-WARD H-BRIDGE MOTOR DRIVER CIRCUIT UTILIZING MOSFET

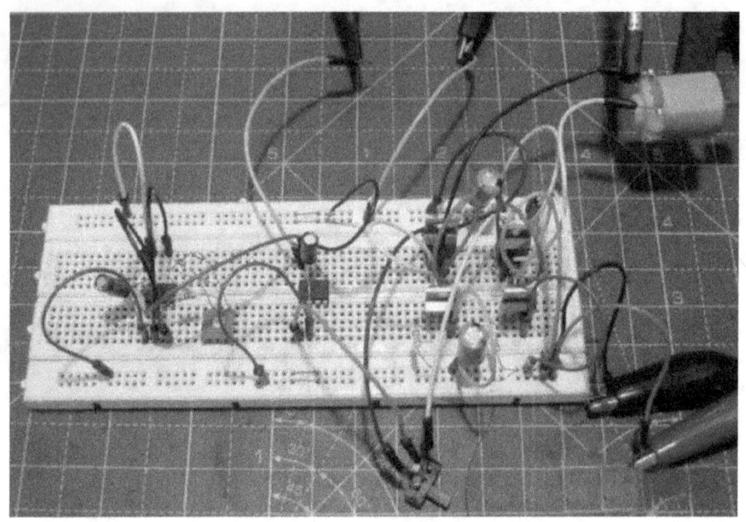

At the beginning driving an engine may appears to be a simple assignment – simply connect the engine to the fitting voltage rail and it will begin turning. In any situation, this isn't the ideal method to drive an engine particularly when there are different segments associated with the circuit. Here we will talk about the most ordinarily utilized and effective approach to drive DC engines - H-Bridge circuit.

Motor Driving

The most widely recognized sort of engine you may run over in specialist hovers for low power applications is the 3V DC engine demonstrated as follows. This sort of engine is upgraded for low voltage activity from two 1.5V cells.

Furthermore, running it is as straightforward as associating it to two cells – the engine starts up in a split second and runs long as the batteries are associated. While this sort of arrangement is useful for 'static' applications like a little windmill or fan, with regards to a 'dynamic' application like robots, more exactness is required – as factor speed as well as torque control.

Clearly diminishing the voltage over the engine diminishes the speed and a dead battery brings about a moderate engine however on the off chance that the engine is controlled from a rail normal to more than one gadget, an appropriate driving circuit is required.

This can even be as a variable straight controller like the LM317 – the voltage over the engine can be fluctuated to speed up. In case increasingly current is required, this circuit can be fabricated tactfully with a couple of bipolar transistors. The greatest downside with this sort of arrangement is the proficiency – simply like with some other burden, the transistor scatters all the undesirable power.

The answer for this issue is a strategy called PWM or heartbeat width tweak. Here, the engine is driven by a square wave with a customizable obligation cycle (the proportion of on time to the time of the sign). The all out power conveyed is relative to the obligation cycle. As it were, the engine is controlled for a little part of the timespan – so after some time the normal capacity to the engine is low. With a 0% obligation cycle, the engine is off (no present streaming); with an obligation cycle of half the engine runs at half power (a wide portion of the present draw) and 100% speaks to full power at most extreme current draw.

This is actualized by interfacing the engine high side and driving it with a N-channel MOSFET, which is driven again by a Pulse Width Modulation signal.

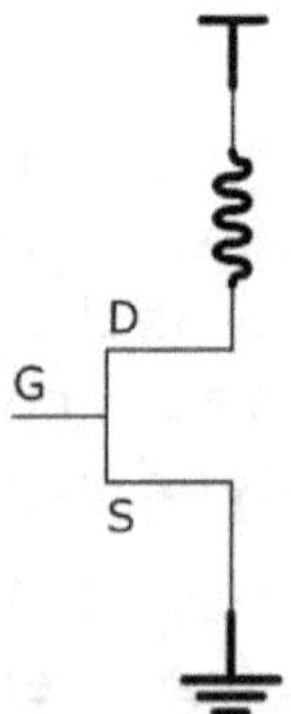

N-Channel PWM Motor Driver

This makes them intrigue suggestions – a 3V engine can be driven utilizing a 12V stockpile utilizing a low obligation cycle since the engine sees just the normal voltage. With cautious plan, this takes out the requirement for a different engine control supply.

Imagine a scenario in which we have to switch the course of the engine. This is done by exchanging the engine terminals, however this should be possible electrically.

One choice could be to utilize another FET and a negative stock to switch bearings. This requires one terminal of the engine to be forever grounded as well as the other associated with either the positive or negative stock. Here, the MOSFETs demonstration like a SPDT switch.

Be that as it may, an increasingly exquisite arrangement exists.

The H-Bridge Motor Driver Circuit

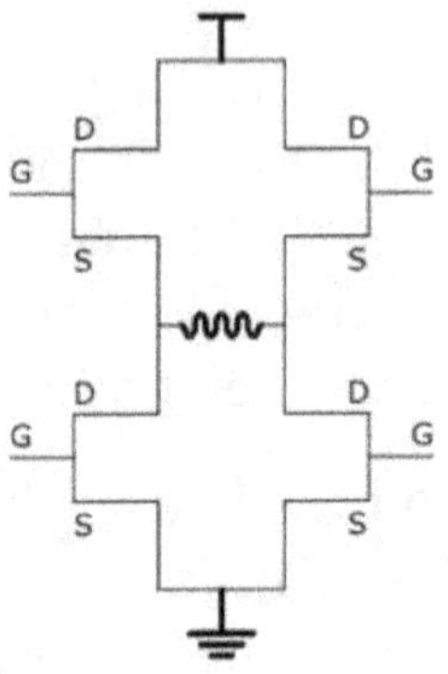

This circuit is called H-connect in light of the fact that the MOSFETs structure the two vertical strokes and the engine frames the level stroke of the letters in order 'H'. It is the basic and rich answer for all engine driving issues. The bearing can be changed effectively and the speed can be controlled.

In a H-connect setup, just the askew inverse sets of MOSFETs are initiated to control the course, as appeared in the underneath figure:

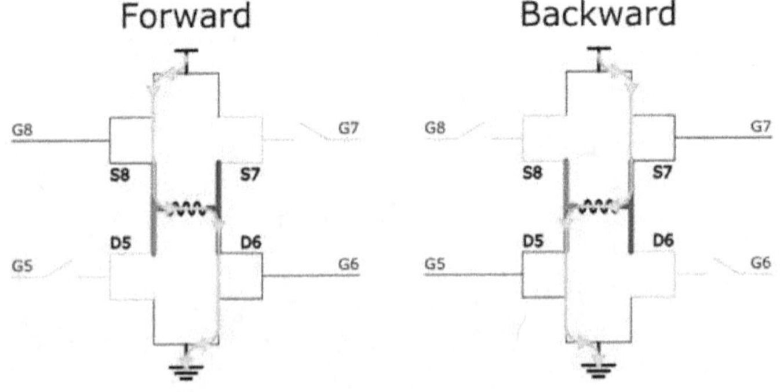

When enacting one sets of (corner to corner inverse) MOSFETs, the engine sees current stream one way as well as when the other pair is actuated, the current across the engine turns around heading.

The MOSFETs can be left on for full power or PWM-ed for control guideline or killed to allow the engine to stop. Initiating both base and top MOSFETs (however never together) brakes the engine.

Another approach to execute H-Bridge is utilizing 555 clocks, which we talked about in past instructional exercise.

Components Required

For the H-Bridge

- DC engine

- 2x IRF5210 P-channel MOSFETs generally equal

- 2x IRF3205 N-channel MOSFETs generally equal

- 2x 100uF electrolytic capacitors (decoupling)

- 2x 10K resistors (pulldown)

- 2x 100nF fired capacitors (decoupling)

For the Control Circuit

- 1x 555 clock (any variation, ideally CMOS)
- 2x 1N4148 generally some other sign/ultra-fast diode
- 1x TC4427 generally any fitting door driver
- 1x 1K resistor (timing)
- 1x 10K potentiometer (timing)
- 4.7uF capacitor (decoupling)
- 4.7nF capacitor (timing)
- Ten uF electrolytic capacitor (decoupling)
- 100nF earthenware capacitor (decoupling)
- SPDT switch

Schematics for Simple H-Bridge Circuit

Since we have the hypothesis off the beaten path, it's an ideal opportunity to get our hands grimy and fabricate a H-connect engine driver. This circuit has enough capacity to drive medium evaluated engines to 20A and 40V with legitimate development and heatsinking. A few highlights have been improved, similar to the utilization of a SPDT change to control the course.

Likewise, the high side MOSFETs are P-channel for straightforwardness. With the proper driving circuit (with bootstrapping), N-channel MOSFETs could likewise be utilized.

The total circuit outline for this H-Bridge utilizing MOSFETs is given underneath:

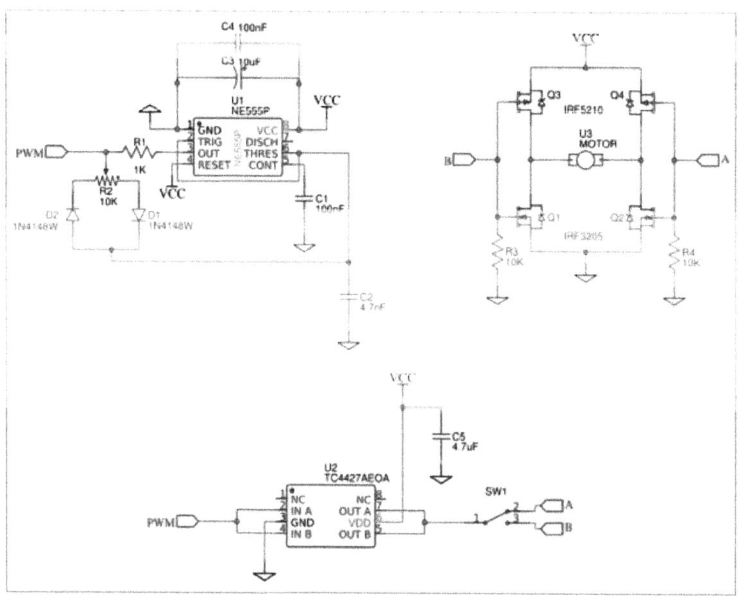

Working Explanation

1. The 555 Timer

The clock is a basic 555 circuit that creates an obligation cycle from around 10% to 90%. The recurrence is set by R1, R2 as well as C2. High frequencies are wanted to decrease discernible whimpering, however this likewise implies an all the more dominant door driver is required. The obligation cycle is constrained by potentiometer R2. Get familiar with utilizing 555 clock in astable mode here.

This circuit can be supplanted by some other PWM source like an Arduino.

2. Entryway Driver

The entryway driver is a standard two-channel TC4427, with 1.5A sink/source per channel. Here, both the channels have been //ed for all the more driving current. Once more, if the recurrence is higher the entryway driver should be all the more dominant.

The SPDT switch is utilized to choose the leg of the H-connect which controls the bearing.

3. H-Bridge

This is the working piece of the circuit that controls the engine. The MOSFET doors are ordinarily pulled low by the pulldown resistor. This outcomes in both the P-channel MOSFETs turning on, however this isn't an issue since no current can stream. At the point when the Pulse Width Modulation signal is applied to the doors of one leg, the N as well as P-channel MOS-FETs are turned on as well as off at the same time, controlling the power.

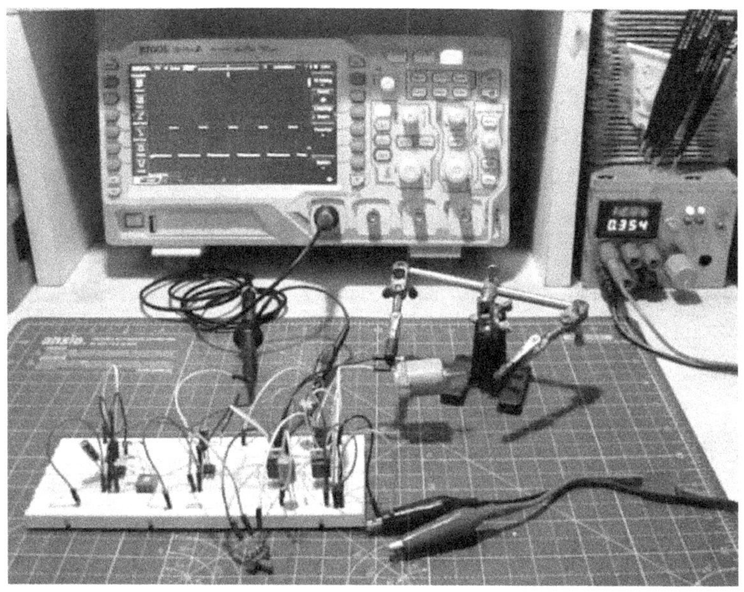

H-Bridge Circuit Construction Tips

The greatest bit of leeway of this circuit is that it very well may be scaled to drive engines everything being equal, and not just engines – whatever else that needs a bidirectional current sign, similar to sine wave inverters.

When utilizing this circuit even at low powers, legitimate restricted decoupling is an unquestionable requirement except if you need your circuit to be glitchy.

Additionally, if developing this circuit on an increasingly changeless stage like a PCB, a huge ground plane is suggested, getting the low current parts far from the high present ways.

So this basic H-Bridge circuit is the answer for some, engine driving issues like bidirectionally, control the board and proficiency.

19. RECURRENCE TO VOLTAGE CONVERTER CIRCUIT

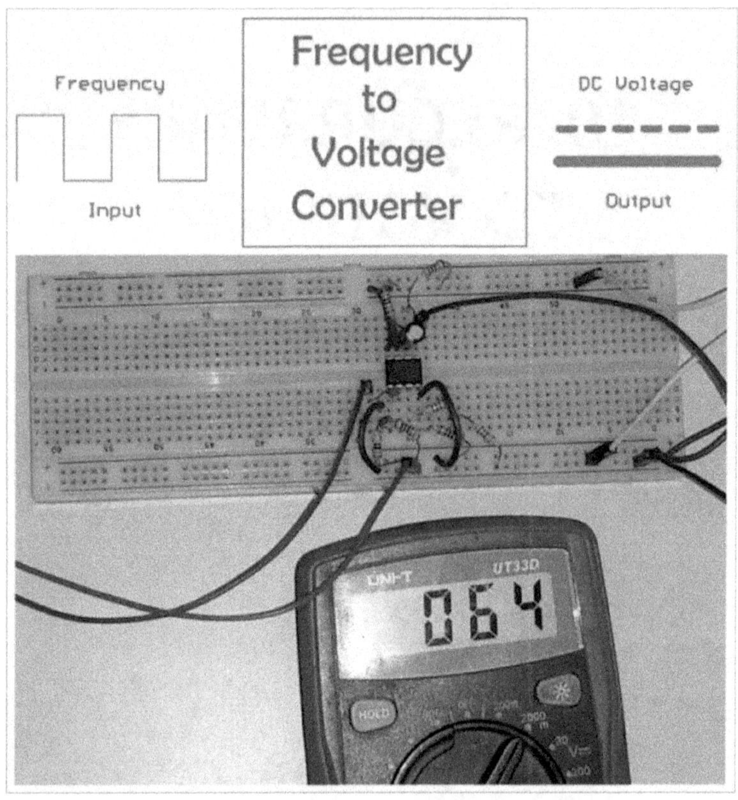

Recurrence to voltage converter changes over the frequencies or heartbeats to the relative electrical yield, for example, voltage or flow. It is a significant device for electromechanical estimations where rehashed occasions are happening. In this way, when we give a recurrence over a recurrence to voltage converter circuit, it will give a relative DC yield. We are utilizing KA331 IC to assemble a recurrence to voltage converter circuit.

KA331 IC

KA331 is a voltage to recurrence converter which is utilized to make a basic minimal effort simple to computerized converter, yet it can likewise be utilized as a recurrence to voltage converter. The 8 pin DIP IC can work in a wide scope of transmission capacity from 1Hz to 100 KHz. It likewise has a wide scope of supply voltage from 5V to 40V. KA331 is the proportionate to well known LM331. LM331 can likewise be utilized this F-to-V circuit.

The following is pin graph and inward circuit of the KA331 taken from the datasheet,

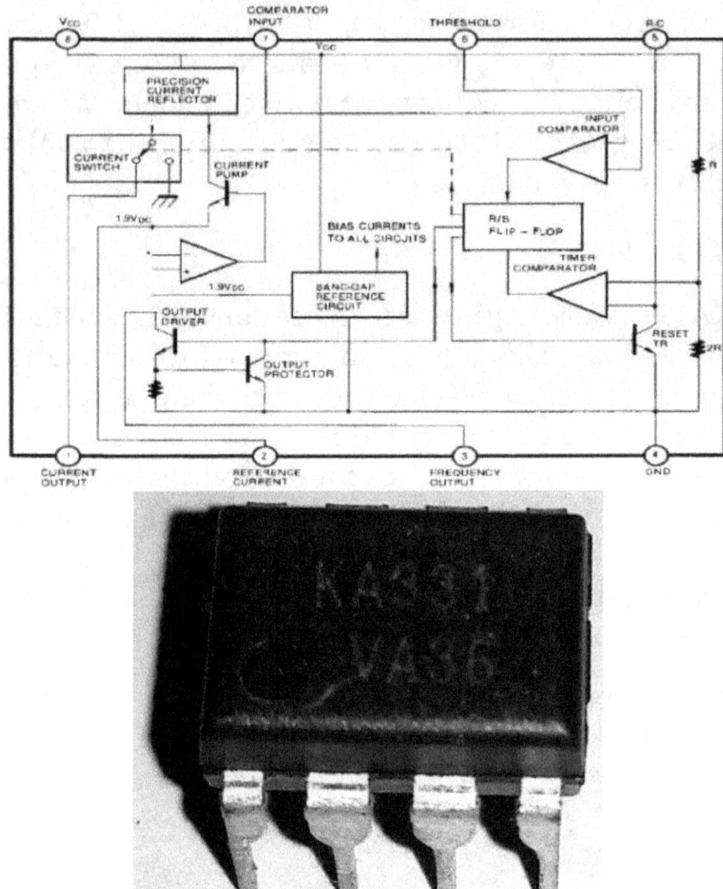

Required Material

- KA331 IC - 1pc
- .01uF ceramic capacitor - 1pc
- 470pF ceramic capacitor - 1pc
- 1uF Electrolytic capacitor with a 16V rating
- 10k resistor with 1% stability rating MFR -

2pcs
- 100k resistor with 1% stability rating MFR - 2pcs
- A 68k resistor with 1% stability rating MFR - 1pc
- A 6.8k resistor with 1% stability rating MFR - 1pc
- Breadboard
- 15V power supply
- Single strand wire
- A frequency generator or function generator to check the overall circuit.

Schematic diagram

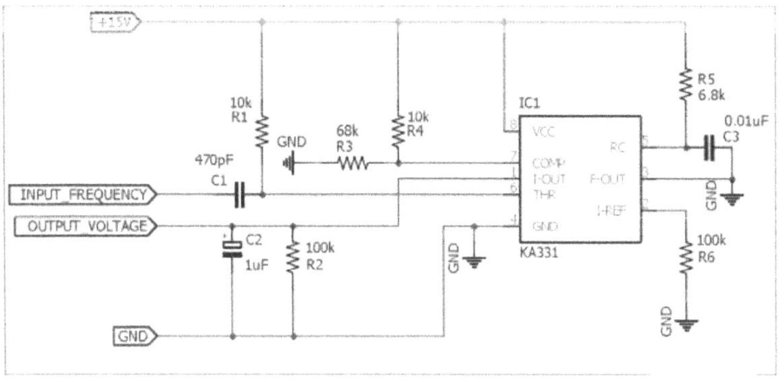

Working of Frequency to Voltage Circuit

The fundamental segment of the circuit is KA331. The contribution of the circuit is associated over a 470pF capacitor C1, which is additionally associated with the limit pin of KA331 (pin 6). Resistor R3 as well as R4 are shaping the Voltage Divider Circuit which is associated with Comparator PIN 7 of KA331. Capacitor C3 and Resistor R5 is the RC clock which gives the necessary swaying over the pin 5. Resistor R2 is giving the reference current over the pin 2. The circuit is given by 15v voltage which is associated over the pin 8 of KA331.

To figure the yield voltage of the circuit, the recipe is –

$$\textbf{Vout} = \textbf{f}_{\textbf{input}} \textbf{ x Reference voltage x } (\textbf{R}_{\textbf{L}}/\textbf{R}_{\textbf{S}}) \textbf{ x } (\textbf{R}_{\textbf{t}} \textbf{ x C}_{\textbf{t}})$$

Where finput is the recurrence, RL is the heap resistor, RS is the present source resistor, Rt and Ct is the resistor and capacitor of the RC oscillator.

In this way, for our circuit, the recipe will be –

$$\textbf{Vout} = \textbf{f}_{\textbf{input}} \textbf{ x Reference voltage x } (\textbf{R}_{\textbf{6}}/\textbf{R}_{\textbf{2}}) \textbf{ x } (\textbf{R}_{\textbf{5}} \textbf{ x C}_{\textbf{3}})$$

According to the datasheet, the reference voltage of KA331 is 1.89V. Thus, in the event that we give 500 Hz of info signal over the circuit to get the yield voltage –

$$\textbf{Vout} = \textbf{500 x 1.89 x (100k/100k) x (6.8k x 0.001uf)}$$

Vout = 500 x 1.89 x 1 x (6800k x 10^{-8})

Vout = 0.064V or 64mV

In this way, When a 500 Hz recurrence applied over the circuit, the circuit will give 64 mV yield.

We have developed the circuit on the breadboard.

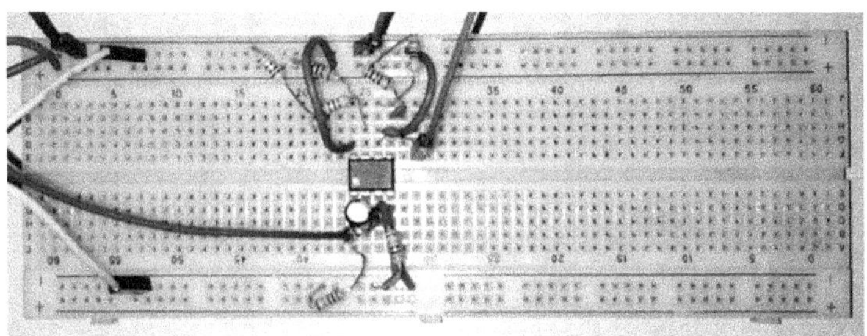

Testing of Frequency to Voltage Circuit

To test the circuit, following devices are utilized –

- Logical PSD3205 seat control supply.

- Metravi FG3000 work generator.

- UNI-T UT33D multimeter.

The circuit is developed utilizing 1% Metal Film Resistors and the capacitors resiliences are not considered. The room temperature was 22 degree Celsius during the testing.

To test the circuit, the seat control supply is set at the 15V yield.

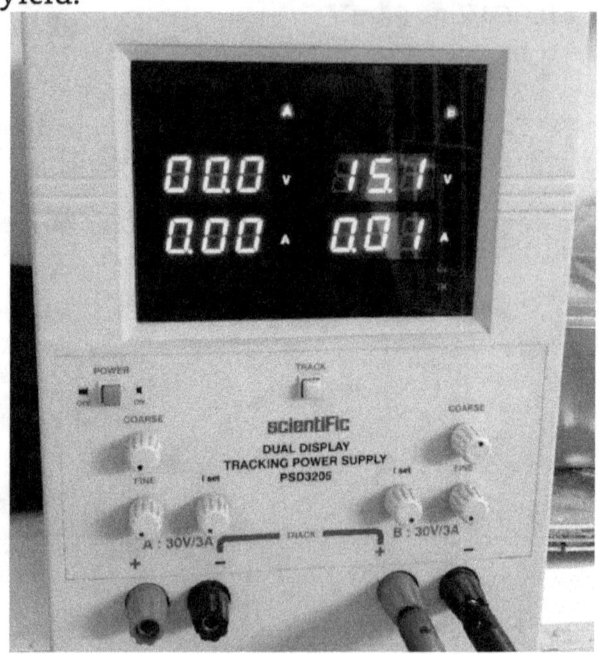

The Function generator is giving approx 500 Hz as a square wave yield.

For the individuals who don't approach the capacity generator, a clock circuit can be developed utilizing the great LM555 IC or an Arduino can likewise be utilized to fabricate work generator. However, the Android application can likewise work where sign are created through the earphone yield.

The Multi-meter is associated over the yield and the range is chosen as mili-volt.

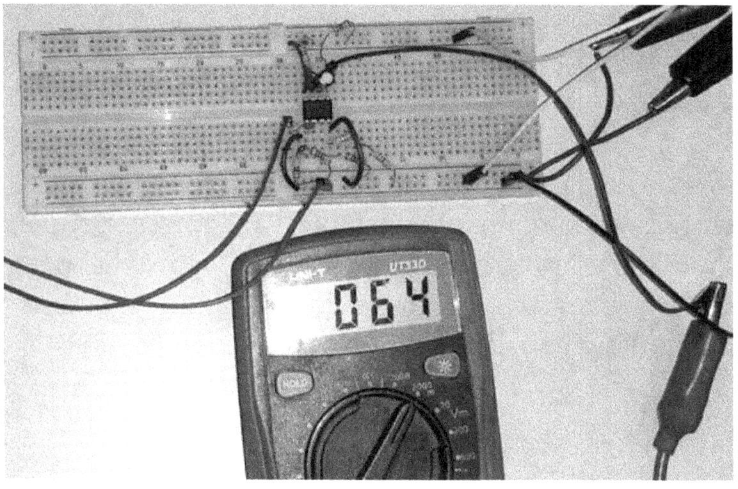

The yield of the multimeter is demonstrating the determined worth. The circuit is giving 64 mV yield when 500 Hz square wave is provided over the information.

The point by point working different information sources are given and the yield voltage is changed in the proportion of the info voltage.

Improvements

This Frequency to Voltage Converter Circuit can be built on a PCB for better precision. The basic area of the circuit is the RC oscillator. The RC oscillator should be set in a nearby separation over the KA331 IC. In long separation, the copper follow could float the wavering as it will include extra obstruction and furthermore contribute stray capacitance. The best possible Ground plane is additionally required.

Applications

Recurrence to voltage converter is utilized in estimations and instrumentation like Tachometer utilizes Frequency to voltage converter to compute the speed of an engine. Diverse sort of check meters, speedometers likewise utilize this procedure.

20. MISSING PULSE DETECTOR CIRCUIT

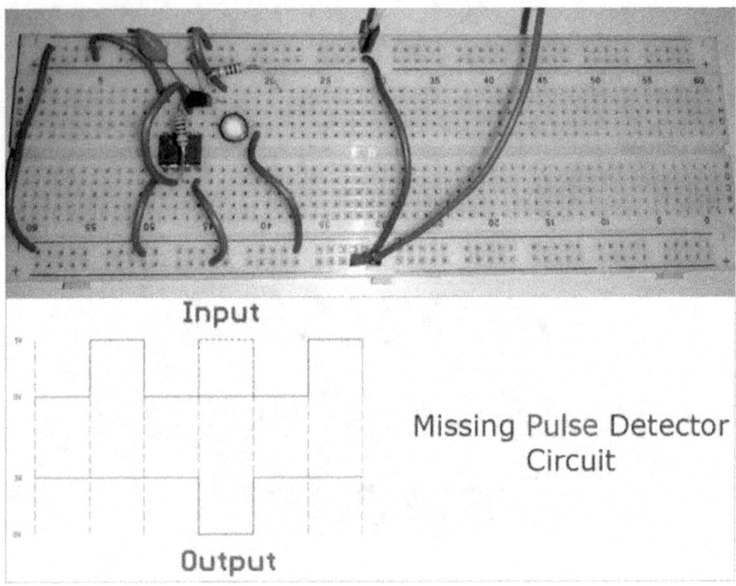

At the point when a sign experiences an abrupt change from base an incentive to higher worth and again comes to base an incentive from higher incentive after some time. It is called a Pulse signal.

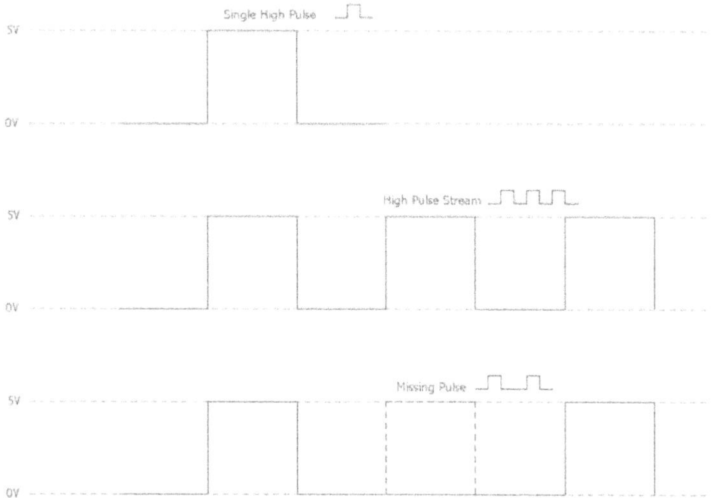

In above picture, the principal waveform shows a solitary heartbeat where the sign is changing from 0 to 5v (low to high) and 5v to 0 (high to low) inside a brief timeframe. Second waveform shows a surge of 5-volt beats in the sign line. Presently when a portion of the beats in this heartbeat bind are neglected to happen which are having the predefined interim time, a Missing Pulse Detector Circuit is required to distinguish those missing heartbeats. The identifier circuit is fit to give missing heartbeat warning. Last waveform appeared in the picture is a missing heartbeat signal.

Here we will construct a Simple Missing Pulse Detector Circuit with not many parts.

Required Components

1. Breadboard

2. 555 clock IC

3. 2 pcs 10k resistors

4. BC337 NPN Bipolar Junction Transistor

5. Single strand wires for the association in the bread-board.

6. 0.01uF artistic plate capacitor

7. 0.1uF artistic plate capacitor

8. Voltage wellspring of 12 volt/500 mA (An Adapter can be utilized)

We need barely any different things to test Missing Pulse Detector Circuit:

1. Any sort of drive button (In this task, the material switch is utilized to interfere with the information heartbeats.)

2. A source which gives persistent and stable heart-beats.

It tends to be a capacity generator or any sort of square wave or triangular wave source.

3. An oscilloscope to quantify the yield.

555 Timer IC

555 Timer IC is a great clock IC which can be utilized in numerous sorts of timing related applications,

check all the 555 Timer Circuit here. This is a eight pin IC. The pin chart of the 555 clock IC is appeared in the underneath picture.

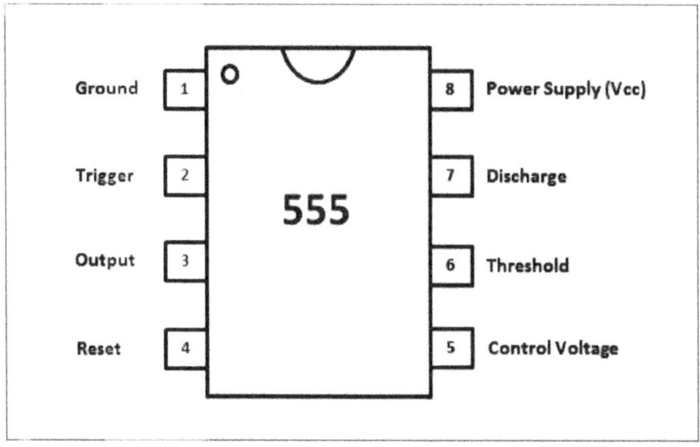

BC337 NPN Transistor

Transistor BC337 is a NPN bipolar intersection transistor. It isn't important to explicitly utilize this transistor here, any NPN transistor can be utilized. The transistor BC337 comprises of 3 pins, base, producer, and authority as appeared in below picture:

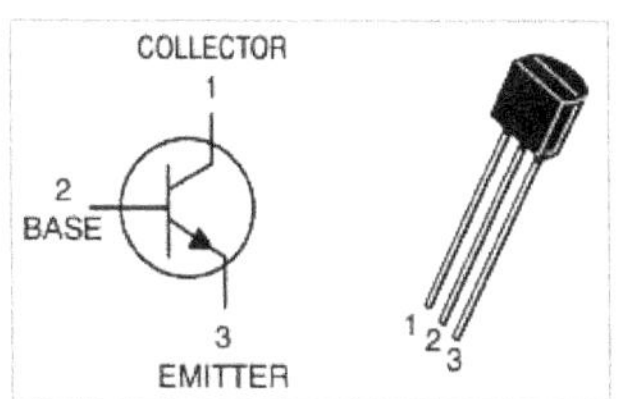

Circuit Diagram

Schematic for Missing Pulse Detector Circuit is demonstrated as follows:

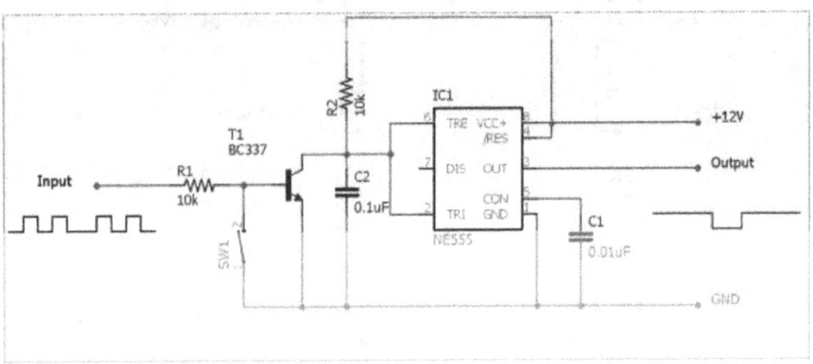

Here the information is associated with the base of BC337 transistor through a 10k resistor. The 555 clock IC associations are likewise in the schematic. The Capacitor C1 is associated in parallel of the transistor T1. The switch SW1 is utilized for the testing reason and to give a missed heartbeat.

Circuit is built on breadboard as appeared in underneath picture:

Working of Missing Pulse Detector Circuit

555 Timer iC is arranged as a monostable heartbeat generator. 555 IC requires a RC oscillator to produce the beats, which is shaped utilizing resistor R2 as well

as capacitor C1. Estimations of R2 and C1 decides the timeframe in monostable mode. Transistor BC337 is associated over the capacitor C1. Information signal is straightforwardly associated with the trigger pin of the clock IC 555 and furthermore associated with the transistor by utilizing a solitary 10k base resistor.

At the point when the info signal doesn't give any missing heartbeat, the clock IC 555 gives a square wave over the yield.

Presently a missing heartbeat shows up, the transistor T1 gets turned on, and as the capacitor C1 is associated over the transistor, it gets released by the BC337. During this release time, RC oscillator neglects to give the ideal planning interim to the IC 555. Consequently, the yield stays high.

Estimations of resistor R2 and capacitor C1 give the planning control of the hardware.

Testing of Missing Pulse Detector Circuit

To test the circuit, a sign source is required which gives constant heartbeats. Here, the alignment purpose of the oscilloscope is utilized for the information signal source reason.

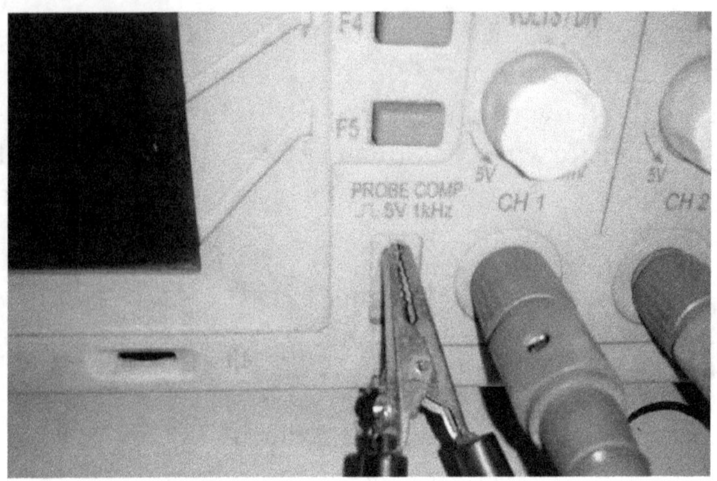

In the above picture, the alignment purpose of the oscilloscope is indicated which give 1Khz square wave in five volts plentifulness.

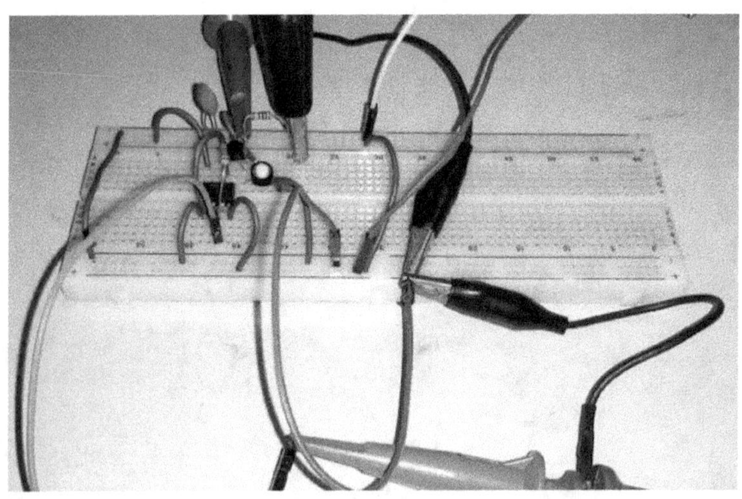

To hinder or to miss the info beats, a material switch is utilized which is associated with the Transistor BC337 base and to the ground.

At whatever point the material switch is being squeezed, the base of the BC337 transistor is being shorted with the ground. Because of this, the transistor kills and the capacitors C1 gets charged.

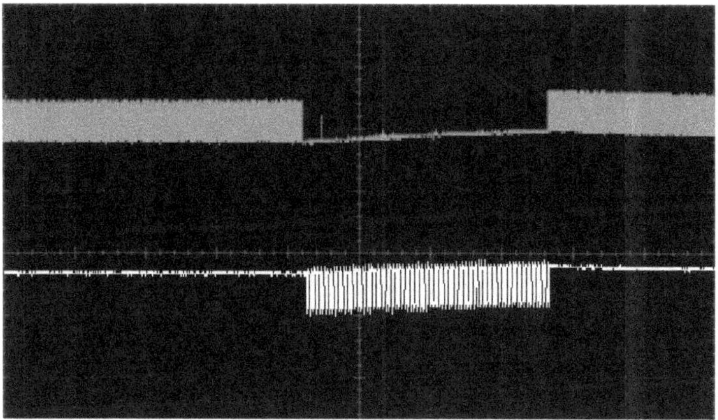

In the above picture, the oscilloscope is giving two sign, Red one is information as well as Yellow 1 is yield. At the point when the switch is squeezed, the beats get missed and the circuit gives square wave at that missed heartbeat time length.

You can additionally check the beneath to see info and yield waveform in the oscilloscope:

Complete working of the Missing Pulse Detector Circuitry is appeared toward the end.

Applications

Missing heartbeat generator circuit is a phenomenal use of the exemplary 555 clock IC. It can trigger a caution or inform the client when there is some end or break in some procedure.

1. Numerous hardware fan framework gives ceaseless heartbeats during the activity. This circuit can without much of a stretch decide and trigger the caution if the fan has been halted or not filling in as it ought to be.

2. In the restorative field, the missing heartbeat indicator circuit is utilized with heartbeat checking gadgets. This could caution the specialists for variations from the norm in the heartbeat.

3. This circuit is likewise exceptionally valuable to recognize a misfortune in exchanging current stock.

4. It can likewise be utilized for half wave or full wave recognition in different sign source estimating related activity.

5. In the modern field where fast identification is required, a missing heartbeat finder can be utilized.

Thank You

www.ingramcontent.com/pod-product-compliance
Lightning Source LLC
Chambersburg PA
CBHW071403150726
48000CB00001B/149